SEDA
STAFF AND EDUCATIONAL
DEVELOPMENT ASSOCIATION

**Staff and Educational
Development Series**

INSPIRING STUDENTS: CASE STUDIES in MOTIVATING THE LEARNER

Stephen Fallows and Kemal Ahmet

**KOGAN
PAGE**

First published in 1999

Kogan Page Limited
120 Pentonville Road
London N1 9JN

British Library Cataloguing in Publication Data

A CIP record for this book is available from the British Library.

ISBN 0 7494 2872 4

Typeset by JS Typesetting, Wellingborough, Northants
Printed and bound by Clays Ltd, St Ives plc

Contents

Notes on Contributors

Dr Kemal Ahmet has a Bachelor's degree in physics, Master's degree in astrophysics and Doctorate in particle physics. He also holds a postgraduate certificate in education. He has been teaching science for 20 years at senior school, college and university level. In addition to being a Principal Teaching Fellow at the University of Luton, he is an associate lecturer at the Open University and has been a subject specialist teaching quality assessor for the Higher Education Funding Council for England (HEFCE).

Dr Jim Aiton is a senior lecturer in the School of Biomedical Sciences at the University of St Andrews where he is also the Co-ordinator of Pre-Honours Teaching and chairs the School's Information Technology Committee. He is actively involved in developing network-based learning support materials for biology and medical science students and has been involved in the development of a number of software packages for teaching. His research interests include the computer-aided 3D reconstruction of histological material.

Dr Josefina Alvarez was born in Spain and raised in Argentina. She has a PhD in mathematics from the University of Buenos Aires, under Alberto P Calderon, and she is currently a Professor of Mathematics at New Mexico State University.

Dr Alvarez tries to maintain a difficult balance between her strong interests in harmonic analysis and in teaching and curriculum development.

In the area of teaching and curriculum development, she has published several papers and she has co-authored a manuscript titled 'Teaching mathematics courses using themes'. This manuscript has been submitted to the Mathematical Association of America. Dr Alvarez has given several talks and workshops at professional meetings and universities, and she has conducted two National Science Foundation short courses for college teachers, at the University of Texas at Austin and at the University of Puerto Rico, founded by the National Science Foundation. She is the 1998 recipient of the El Paso Energy Foundation Faculty Achievement Award, for Outstanding University Teaching.

Anne Arnold is a lecturer in the School of Economics at the University of Adelaide, South Australia. She has a Master's degree in economics, followed a Bachelor's degree in statistics, has worked as a statistician, and now lectures in statistics.

Dr Balasubramanyam Chandramohan is the Field Manager for Post-colonial Studies at the University of Luton. He is a senior lecturer in linguistics at the Faculty of Humanities. He is also the Assistant Course Manager for the MA in

Educational Management (Summer School Delivery). His current research interests include pedagogical issues, especially those that relate to interdisciplinary studies and the use of IT in higher education.

Dr Chandramohan studied at Sri Venkateswara and Jawaharlal Nehru Universities in India and at the University of Sheffield, from where he obtained a Doctorate. He has taught at universities in India, Algeria, Tunisia, Switzerland and the United Kingdom.

Dr Graham Clarke has Bachelor's degrees in biology and mathematics, a Master's degree in computing and a Doctorate in radiological science. He also holds postgraduate certificates in education and in applied statistics, and is currently studying for a Master's degree in applied statistics. His main research interests lie in the field of biometry. Dr Clarke teaches biology and research methodology to undergraduate and postgraduate students in both the science and health faculties of the University of Wales – Bangor. He is at present involved in developing a 'resource-based' course in human biology.

Dr Stephen Fallows is Reader in Educational Development at the University of Luton. This role is research based and a key theme in his work is the evaluation of novel approaches to teaching and course delivery. Dr Fallows made the move to educational development from his original discipline of food policy via the use of computer-based teaching and these are interests that he maintains. Dr Fallows' current responsibilities are principally staff development related and he has a close involvement in the University of Luton's activities for the continuing professional development of academic staff.

John Flynn is a senior lecturer at the University of Lincolnshire and Humberside, in the Hull Business School. He has a Master's degree in statistics and a PGCE, and over 15 years' experience in the application of statistical and mathematical techniques to toxicology, agriculture and market research as well as the development of training courses to support project management software in the aerospace industry.

He has lectured in quantitative methods on the university's MBA programme, including overseas delivery in Spain, Northern Ireland, Singapore and Oman. Undergraduate quantitative methods courses for business studies students have been recently enhanced by the design and implementation of multiple-choice questions with feedback, funded by the university's BP project to supplement undergraduate teaching.

Dr Philip Hammond is a Reader in the School of Evolutionary and Environmental Biology at the University of St Andrews and is the current Director of the Sea Mammal Research Unit, which has recently relocated to St Andrews from Cambridge. He is the organizer of the Quantitative Methods in Biology course and is responsible for preparing the teaching materials and training the postgraduate tutors. His research interests include computer-intensive methods to estimate marine mammal ecological parameters.

Dr Gareth Hughes is a senior lecturer in the Institute of Ecology and Resource Management at the University of Edinburgh and, since 1996–97, the Course

Organizer for Quantitative Biology. As Assistant Director of the Biology Teaching Organization he was responsible for the implementation of the quantitative biology course in the new School of Biology curriculum in 1992–93. He has taught quantitative methods to biology students since 1977, first at the University of the West Indies, then at the University of Edinburgh. His research centres on the assessment of crop losses to diseases, weeds and insect pests.

Professor Calvin S Kalman is a professor in the Department of Physics and a member of the Center for the Study of Classroom Processes at Concordia University in Montreal. He has been active in high-energy physics for 30 years. His work includes the only book on preons and he is currently chair and editor of the proceedings of the international biennial conference series on hyperons, charm and beauty hadrons. Additionally, he has always maintained an interest in exploring educational methods in physics. His early publications were in computer-based learning. Recently he has written on and given workshops on various aspects of the student-centred classroom.

Dr Jonathan Lean is a lecturer within the Business, Economics and Management Department of the University of Plymouth Business School. He has a PhD in small business management and policy and has published widely in the area of small business and entrepreneurship. Dr Lean's current teaching responsibilities include courses in computer information systems, business strategy and business operations. He has a SEDA-accredited qualification in teaching and learning.

Terry Mangles is a principal lecturer within the Business, Economics and Management Department of the University of Plymouth Business School. His main areas of expertise are statistics and the development of computer-based information systems. He teaches in quantitative methods, management decision making and computer information systems at both undergraduate and postgraduate level. Mr Mangles works within the DTI-sponsored Plymouth Teaching Company Centre.

Ian McPherson is a teaching fellow, and programme leader for the BSc (Hons) Industrial Design course, at Napier University, Edinburgh, Scotland. He studied industrial design at Glasgow School of Art and also holds a postgraduate teaching qualification from Jordanhill College of Education. His 30 years' experience of teaching ranges from secondary school to undergraduate and postgraduate university levels. He continues to maintain an interest in practising as a designer.

Jonathan Moizer is a lecturer within the Business, Economics and Management Department of the University of Plymouth Business School. He is currently completing a PhD in systems dynamics computer modelling. His current teaching responsibilities are largely in the areas of computer information systems and business technology. He has a SEDA-accredited qualification in teaching and learning.

Dr Susan Nichols is an academic adviser, lecturer and educational researcher with the Flinders University of South Australia. She comes to higher education from a background of teaching English at secondary school level. As an academic adviser, she works with students to improve their literacy skills in subjects across the curriculum. She conducts research in the field of literacy education at all levels.

Dr Ian Nimmo is a senior lecturer in the Department of Biochemistry (of which he is currently head) at the University of Edinburgh. He was for a time organizer of the quantitative biology course and was involved in its development. He has also both developed and organized courses for dental, medical and science students. His current research field is the metabolism of exercise.

Peter Ommundsen is an instructor in the Department of Environmental Sciences at Selkirk College in British Columbia, where he trains wildlife technicians and teaches university biology. He is a Certified Wildlife Biologist (US) and a Registered Professional Biologist (Canada). He has received teaching excellence awards from the United States and Canada.

Carol Primrose worked at Glasgow University Library for 22 years, latterly as senior assistant librarian with special responsibilities for staff training, archaeology, reader instruction and overseas students. She taught information and study skills to a wide range of students from first-year undergraduate to postgraduate research. She was one of a team responsible for producing computer-assisted multimedia learning packages on information and study skills, under the TLTP initiative. In addition, she has developed a training workshop 'Working with Overseas Students' which addresses problems of communication and cultural misunderstanding and which has been presented at several UK universities. She was subject specialist in archaeology and is secretary of the Glasgow Archaeological Society. She is now a training consultant.

Dr John R Savery completed his Doctorate at Indiana University in instructional systems technology and is currently teaching undergraduate computer science courses and graduate education courses at DePaul University in Chicago. He is the lead instructional application designer with the Academic Technology Development Group and works with faculty to integrate instructional technology with effective pedagogy.

Mark W Teale is a senior lecturer at the University of Lincolnshire and Humberside. He joined the university in 1993 after spending 15 years as a manager and management consultant for British Coal. He has a Bachelor's degree in engineering, a Master's degree in business and is studying for a Doctorate in education management. His main research interests at present are in the management of institutions of higher education, particularly the management of change.

Dr Andréa Riesch Toepell has a Bachelor's degree in psychology, and Master's and doctorate degrees in applied psychology. She has been working in the field of community health and adult education programme development for the past eight years. She is assistant professor at Brock University in Canada and has taught at the graduate and undergraduate level for the past five years. Currently, Dr Toepell teaches in the areas of community health, health promotion, gender and health, research methods in health sciences, and sexual health education; these courses represent both core and elective courses for the degrees offered in the health studies programme.

John Truran is a PhD student in the Graduate School of Education at the University of Adelaide. He has taught mathematics in secondary schools and mathematics education in universities. His Master's degree focused on the psychological and pedagogical aspects of the teaching of probability. Currently he is analyzing curriculum forces in schools.

Dr AC Lynn Zelmer is a senior lecturer in the Faculty of Informatics and Communications at Central Queensland University. He teaches in both the Bachelor of Information Technology and Bachelor of Multimedia Studies degrees as well as supervising research students at honours and postgraduate levels. An educator who came to computing via educational technology, Dr Zelmer is actively involved in research and development activities in both multimedia and health informatics.

Editors' Introductory Remarks

This book is a essentially a collection of case studies which focus on the issues surrounding the teaching of subjects for which the students concerned may have little intrinsic interest. The book has grown from our interest in, and action research concerning the teaching of science to students whose interests lie in the quite different disciplines centred around the built environment. Those of our students who plan to become architects or building surveyors view the sciences in a quite different manner than those whose primary academic interests lie within physics, chemistry or related disciplines. Since the students' view of the subject is 'non-standard' it has been necessary to adopt a similarly 'non-standard' approach to course delivery, thereby inspiring the students to maximize their learning.

Long discussions with colleagues indicated that the issue was by no means confined to the teaching of science to built environment students. Rather, examples of the issue could be found across most disciplines and in all institutions. The collection of studies which we present here is drawn from a range of subject areas and from universities around the world. The contributing authors were recruited to the project by our call for 'expressions of interest' which was placed onto a number of e-mail discussion lists originating in the United Kingdom, the United States and Australia. Our call sought to identify university teachers who had faced and overcome the problem of 'teaching students who don't want to learn your subject' and this phrase was used as a working title in the very many e-mail messages which have been sent around the globe during the book's preparation. Throughout the project, our contact with the contributors has been solely by e-mail, except for our one local colleague (who, incidentally, was the last to deliver his contribution!). We have met very few of the contributors face to face. While our contributors are drawn from a wide variety of higher education institutions, the common element is the fact that all are practitioners and the cases described are each drawn from their own practical experiences as teachers.

While each chapter has been created from work within the teaching of a particular subject to a specified group of students, there are always transferable lessons to be learnt. We consider that the transfer of sound approaches and good ideas between subject disciplines is, at least, as important as their transfer between institutions.

Our working title 'Teaching students who don't want to learn your subject' was a very useful 'hook' with which to catch the attention of university teachers around the world (although one cynic observed that this phrase could, from her personal experience, be applied to *all* students). Reading the contributions led us to the conclusion that every one of the authors was inspiring their students and in turn these enlivened, motivated students were inspiring their teachers. This led to the final main title of *Inspiring Students*; and hence, this is deliberately intended to have dual meaning. The sub-title remained open to debate for much longer and our final choice was suggested by one of our contributors, Andréa Toepell. Several other contributors made suggestions but we felt that *Case studies in motivating the learner* summarized perfectly our intentions when originating this project.

Stephen Fallows and Kemal Ahmet
University of Luton, January 1999

1

Inspiring Students: An Introduction

Stephen Fallows and Kemal Ahmet

Inspiring students to become independent and well-motivated learners is perhaps the key role of any educator. A person may nominally become a 'lecturer' by merely standing in front of a class and delivering an oration but to become an educator takes a good deal more. Educators must not only transfer factual items of knowledge and introduce the key debates of the subject to students, they must also deliver enthusiasm and influence students to learn. Similarly, it is clear that students are most inspired and motivated to learn when lecturers are seen to be caring and have genuine concern for learners.

In some exceptional educational contexts, the educator is lucky enough to be presented with groups of students who all arrive for classes already fired with enthusiasm for the subject, with well-developed study skills and with a strong aptitude and ability for academic learning. In such circumstances, the educator's task is to maintain this enthusiasm and to utilize it to ensure that these advanced students achieve the high levels of success and performance suggested by the profile described.

For many more educators, the circumstances are quite different. Students arrive for classes without an enthusiasm for the subject. Their study skills may be underdeveloped. Their track record as academic learners may be less than impressive. In this situation, the task is to develop or even create the enthusiasm for learning. However, as with the more enthusiastic students, the educator's task remains that of maximizing the learning achieved by the students.

Of course, the scenarios described represent the extremes for each of the three parameters considered (subject interest, study skills and academic aptitude). In practice, educators face students located somewhere along the continuum from mediocrity to excellence, and it is generally the case that the group will not be homogeneous but rather will include a range of interest, skills and aptitude.

This book has its primary focus on the first parameter – subject interest – and draws upon the practical experience of colleagues faced with students whose level of interest in their subject matter tends towards the minimal. It also has a particular focus on higher education at university or college level (that is, with older learners and with those who have generally displayed some

1

aptitude for academic learning). However, many of the ideas presented in the case studies have relevance to colleagues in the other phases of education.

Student lack of interest in the subject taught is not uncommon and arises widely throughout the educational system. In the years of compulsory education it is a matter of constant concern since students will always be faced with a wide-ranging curriculum designed to provide a well-rounded education; inevitably this will include, for each student, the personally favoured subjects and those which are less so. As the student progresses into post-compulsory education there will be a concentration onto a narrower curriculum which reflects the student's interests in a chosen academic discipline or career pathway but the problem of the less well-liked aspects continue.

Within higher education, the issue arises because there is often a need to underpin the teaching in the student's chosen discipline with a range of supporting material. Perhaps the most common manifestation of this is the need for students of a wide range of disciplines to be able to manipulate numerical data. It often comes as a surprise for students to learn that (for example) to study biology requires an appreciation of mathematics and statistics; it is not unusual for a student to have chosen biology rather than the other sciences in order to escape numerical analysis.

To teach the supporting subjects will often require greater skills in education than does the teaching of the subject that is the students' primary interest. Particularly successful teaching will almost inevitably require the adoption of a different approach to the teaching and learning activities undertaken; the case studies presented in this book provide a range of examples.

Motivation

Inspiring students is primarily a matter of motivation. When inspired, the students are motivated to engage with the subject and to learn.

An individual's motivation to learn is determined by a range of factors; the following list provides some examples and is by no means complete, and it is not presented in a manner intended to indicate a hierarchy of importance:

- the learner's desire to please the teacher;
- perceived need for the material presented;
- each learner's degree of interest in the subject material;
- the personal philosophical values and beliefs of the learner;
- the learner's attitudes towards the materials being delivered;
- the academic and career aspirations of the learner;
- incentives and rewards which are expected to accrue from the learning.

The relative importance of the different factors suggested in the list will vary over time and with circumstance. For instance, the desire to please the teacher is generally strong in young children but can be non-existent in adult learners.

By contrast, adult learners are much more likely to question the need for the material being delivered and will often be strongly influenced by personal beliefs and aspirations.

In order to maximize learning, it is the educator's task to maximize the positive attributes of each of the factors mentioned:

- *Desire to please:* the key action for the educator is the use of positive and encouraging feedback. The nature of this feedback will vary with circumstance and will range from non-verbal communication (such as smiles and nods of the head) through oral praise (using encouraging words such as 'good' or 'excellent' as appropriate) to formal written comments on written work. Praise, as a tool to inspire students, is particularly effective if directly linked to the student's achievement of a specified learning outcome. For the less motivated student, there is also benefit in focusing praise on the effort put in since this will reinforce the link between the work undertaken and the achievement of the desired outcome. The key requirement is to build the understanding that achievement is not merely a matter of luck or a preordained inevitability.

- *Perceived need:* it is always more pleasant to study topics which are seen to be relevant. In many cases, students can be inspired to learn merely by use of a very clear briefing session which places the topic into the context of the wider programme of work – this gives the students a reason to be motivated. However, indicating the relevance of the topic is just the first step; it is also desirable that the material be delivered within a framework that utilizes examples appropriate to the students' needs. It ought to be obvious that statistics classes which cite examples from the biological sciences are inappropriate for economics students while financial examples are not well received by those with interests in the biological sciences. If the statistics class has to be delivered to a mixed group, then examples taken from everyday life have a common currency for all. Perceived need can also be considered from the perspective of that which is required of the student. Clearly defined course objectives and clearly specified assessed work assist the students to recognize what is required from them and this in turn provides the focus needed for achievement.

- *Degree of interest:* this follows on from the preceding point. If it is recognized that the level of student interest is likely to be low, then the educator will benefit from an exploration of teaching methodologies that seek to involve the student in active learning. Lectures have their place in the portfolio of teaching methodologies but are least effective where the level of subject interest is low; physical attendance rates may be poor and intellectual attentiveness may be limited. A number of the case studies presented later in this book provide examples of how active learning sessions which demand involvement can lead to a raising of the degree of interest.

- *Values and beliefs:* recognition of the diverse nature of the student body can help to ensure that students are inspired to learn. Diversity of values and beliefs can include reference to ethnicity/race, religious beliefs, gender considerations and ethical matters. Group-based learning activities provide affiliations between students in which there is a need to collaborate for the common good regardless of personal values and beliefs. Indeed, debates within the groups that draw upon these values and beliefs can be channelled to make a significant contribution to the learning process.

- *Attitudes:* these build on the previous point but will include the social dimensions that arise from the individual's experience of society. In this context there is a need also to appreciate the differences in attitudes which arise through academic study; there can be quite noticeable differences in attitudes between those students whose primary focus is within the fundamental sciences and those whose academic home is within the humanities. These attitudes tend to have significant influence on the approach to study and should be taken fully into account.

- *Aspirations:* what is the student seeking from the course? Is the student questing after knowledge or merely seeking a qualification? In too many cases, we have to recognize that students are merely seeking academic credit for progression or graduation. For such students, the desire for learning is minimal and confined to that which will be formally assessed. Once such a situation is recognized, it is common practice to address the matter through the assessment process by the use of learning tasks which build through the course to the delivery of a final grade on completion.

- *Incentives and rewards:* for academic study the traditional primary reward is the award of the degree (or other qualification as appropriate). The certificated qualification has been seen by many students as the easy passport to well-paid employment but increasingly it is recognized that the mere acquisition of a degree is not enough. The period of academic life is nowadays considered by many to be an opportunity to develop (through study of a chosen discipline) a range of skills for life such as communications, problem solving, use of information technology and the social skills of group working. Encouraging students towards mastery of these skills can often result in them being inspired to raise the level of general academic performance.

Inspiration in practice

The case studies in this book are all examples of inspiration in practice. The principles discussed above are applied in a range of disciplines. The case studies illustrate the benefits of:

- clear communication of learning objectives and desired outcomes;
- active learning tasks;
- use of positive feedback;
- appropriately focused examples;
- targeted assessment procedures.

Each case study is drawn from the personal experience of teachers within higher education and is presented in a manner from which it is hoped that readers will be able to draw inspiration regardless of their discipline.

CONCLUSION

It must be recognized that 'inspiring students' is not a one-way process. The educator who can inspire students to learn will always gain personal and professional inspiration from observing students' positive engagement with the subject materials. Students can inspire their teacher – but only if the teacher initiates the process by inspiring them to learn.

2

Experiential Learning Through Practicals

Kemal Ahmet and Stephen Fallows

SUMMARY

The authors illustrate the use of experiential learning in science practicals with reference to their work with students who are studying for a range of degrees spanning architecture, design and building surveying; their interests are primarily within their respective practice-based disciplines.

Each subject requires an understanding of a wide variety of science concepts. However, the basic science needed to provide this understanding is traditionally not popular with the students and is perceived to be difficult. Traditional approaches to science teaching are not effective with students who have a diverse range of prior educational and employment histories. The science teaching must be firmly embedded within their experience and interests and this has been found to provide the inspiration needed.

The teaching method adopted derives from a mix of theoretical models of experiential learning and the authors' own action research. It emphasizes active learning and is designed to relate directly to the learners' practical life experiences. Experiential practicals can take many forms but the key features are that the students' time investment is kept to a minimum and personal ownership of data is generated.

INTRODUCTION

Students in subjects related to the built environment frequently encounter core material which is perceived as being remote from the area of main interest, but which is nevertheless vital to underpinning the mainstream subjects. It is especially in these areas that student motivation needs to be maintained. It is important that such core subjects are delivered within the students' experiences and interests.

There is little doubt that student motivation is greatly enhanced when the learning is active, relevant and resulting from the individual's experience. One aspect of our work has led to the emergence of experiential practicals, which are being incorporated into various science modules. Simply, these practicals require the students to collect (with ease), and use, scientific data from familiar environments. This is in contrast to the orthodox laboratory work where data is obtained (often painstakingly) under highly controlled formal environments. This type of work is helping students enormously not only to become familiar with various new concepts introduced in the courses but to provide them with a feel for the numerical values involved.

The institution

The University of Luton is England's newest university, having been created from the Luton College of Higher Education as recently as 1993. It is a medium-sized university, with some 9000 full-time and 5000 part-time students. The mission statement of the university stresses that courses are characterized by their vocational relevance, and indeed many students' graduate with qualifications of direct relevance their intended work.

The department

The Department of Technology (formerly the Department of the Built Environment) includes students studying for BSc honours degrees in construction management, building surveying, architecture, building technology and interior design. The teaching is multidisciplinary, ranging from subjects such as science and quantitative methods to management, law and design. Around 400 students are studying for degrees within the department. The university's teaching of built environment-related subjects has recently been subjected to external peer evaluation and has been judged to be excellent (HEFCE, 1997).

The modular scheme

The University of Luton operates the largest modular credit scheme in England. Logical groups of modules form fields of study, where particular combinations yield specific degrees. Module levels range from zero (foundation) to three (final year). In principle, students can pick and choose modules from any field; however, this leads to general degrees, having no specific title. In general, the students tend to study mandatory core modules within a given field and to select from a choice of optional modules leading to a specialist degree. It is usual for eight modules to be studied in each of the three years of academic study. For an honours degree a minimum specified number must be at the higher levels, two and three.

The nature and numbers of students

Sizes of groups vary according to the particular course. The built environment field cohort is typically around 100 students per year and includes the students in the disciplines previously mentioned. Students are from a diverse range of prior educational and employment histories where around 40 per cent are classed as mature (that is over 21 years of age on entry) while typically 10 per cent are from overseas. A common curriculum exists for all built environment students in the first year.

The courses

A wide range of subjects is taught within the built environment field. The main areas include:

- science;
- technology;
- mathematics;
- law;
- economics;
- land surveying;
- environmental engineering;
- design and computer-aided design (CAD);
- management principles;
- town planning.

The science components are taught at zero and first level and are essential to lay the foundations for the higher level building technology, environmental engineering and structural design modules.

SCIENCE IN THE CURRICULUM

It is nationally recognized that it is essential for students of the built environment to obtain a grounding in the basics of both physical and materials science, see, for example, CIOB (1994) or Mole (1997). The physical and environmental science curriculum at level one includes lighting, thermal physics, acoustics, fluid flow and electricity. The science of materials consists of studies into elasticity, the strength of materials and a glimpse at other relevant properties such as expansivity, porosity and density. Students are strongly encouraged to read copiously about individual types of materials.

Within the science-based modules, teaching and learning methods include highly interactive lectures, tutorials and laboratory sessions, with the latter occupying around 50 per cent of the formal contact time allocated to teaching and learning.

Problems with teaching science: lack of motivation and interest

A high proportion of students, notably those in architecture and design, traditionally (and incorrectly), feel that the science is not relevant to their discipline. This is not surprising as the teaching is often carried out in abstract, ie out of context and often without the use of context focused practicals or other direct involvement of the students. Common questions asked by students range from 'What is the relevance?' to 'How will this help me in my future career?' Where students see the relevance and can make the connections between theory and the 'real world', the level of interest and enthusiasm improves dramatically.

Action research

Over the past five years, we have employed the processes of action research, one method of reflecting on practice, to periodically introduce and implement new teaching and learning methods and then to monitor the effects on student motivation, interest and learning. The observations have been used as feedback, to make necessary adjustments to the teaching methods. (The principles of action research are explained in, for example, Zuber-Skerritt, 1992). The effectiveness of the experiential practicals has been ascertained using this method. On completion of a given task, direct feedback from students yields crucial information regarding the success of these 'practicals'. The evolution is still taking place at present.

PRACTICAL WORK

Experimentation is at the root of all science work. Theoretical science, too, must always be substantiated by experimental evidence. For this reason, practical work must form an essential ingredient of any respectable science-based course.

Mainstream experimental work

Nationally, students in the pure science subjects (eg physics, biology and chemistry) are typically expected to spend at least 50 per cent of the contact time on laboratory work. In our built environment applied science courses, this emphasis is maintained. Various 'conventional' experiments are carried out by the students. The work is mandatory and no student can achieve a pass without a substantial attendance record in the laboratory.

Students are expected to work in pairs and perform experiments following a 'circuit'. This technique ensures maximum use of resources by rotating students through a series of experiments, each team commencing with a different task. Students carry out six foundation experiments followed by an assortment of six more involved experiments over a period of 12 weeks. The presence of one technician, one demonstrator and a senior member of staff per laboratory provide support. Staff ensure that the equipment is set up and working properly and help students to carry out the work. Students are quizzed in a non-threatening friendly manner to help them learn and understand the work. To emphasize the importance of the experimental work 50 per cent of the total marks for a module are awarded for completion of the laboratory work and the submission of the written records containing the details of the work carried out. The latter is contained in a laboratory logbook where the emphasis is on entering the details simultaneous to the experimental work being carried out.

This conventional type of practical work is performed in the laboratory, i.e. under carefully controlled conditions – indeed this is the very essence of scientific work. The results of such experiments, however, yield values which are obtainable (and repeatable) under tightly controlled conditions. As one example, strength tests on timber are carried out on artificially small 'ideal' samples, that is those without defects such as knots and cracks. Materials used in the real environment are of course far from ideal and very variable. While these conventional types of experiments are essential, they are not always sufficiently 'tangible' for the students. Students frequently fail to appreciate (justifiably) the connection with the 'real world'. It is for this reason that the idea of experiential practicals was introduced.

EXPERIENTIAL PRACTICALS

Various ideas have been tried and tested. In all cases, the emphasis of experiential practicals is on minimizing time expenditure on irrelevant work (such as setting up equipment) and maximizing the relevant experience and hence, learning gained. The main point about experiential practicals is that they are carried out (passively) in everyday environments, which are constantly being experienced. The commonality is that in all cases the data is unique and gathered with ease. Although a high technology approach can be employed, many useful experiential practicals can be carried out with low-cost equipment.

What are experiential practicals?

Experiential practicals are used to collect scientific data from environments familiar to the student. They are designed to help them obtain a grasp of the relevant concepts by using the surroundings of 'experience'. The results of testing students over many years have shown that although students may be able to reproduce material for examinations, they often fail to have the necessary 'feel' for the values of the important physical parameters, so necessary for building professionals.

Students frequently use their own accommodation as the environment for investigation. Familiar parameters for data collection include temperature, relative humidity, sound levels and light levels. The data is often collected using micro-dataloggers, encased in containers the size of 35 mm film canisters. These are so small that they take up negligible space *in situ* and are non-intrusive, simple to install and remove. Monitoring, then, takes place in the environments that the student is continuously experiencing. The time of data collection can range from days to weeks. Shorter lengths of time can be used although cycles of at least one day or one week are desirable to show variations and trends.

How are experiential practicals carried out?

Following the introduction of the concept in the formal teaching and learning sessions, students are provided with the appropriate details and hardware to carry out the tests. For example, when the concepts connected with human comfort levels have been introduced, students are provided with basic instructions and the appropriate dataloggers for installation into their own chosen experiential environments. Installation merely involves the placement into a suitable location for the required period. The student needs to think carefully about the location for generating typical data; even this phase results in important learning. We have consistently observed that students take the installation (and return) very seriously; to date, there have been no incidents of lost or damaged equipment.

At the end of the 'experimental' period, students return the dataloggers for transfer of data, which is usually downloaded into a computer. Results are then printed out in tabular form or further processed. The most effective method for observing results and learning from them is to use the graphical form of presentation (see Figure 2.1). First, the individual interprets charts; this is followed by small group discussion. This analysis stage is crucial. To follow, results are presented and discussed in larger groups. For a given set of data, the students look for maximum and minimum values, trend lines, peculiarities and anomalies. As the results are studied, connections are inevitably made with the environment of experience and reasons for the variations are produced. Clearly, some of the trends are caused by external/natural influences (eg weather) while the occupants (eg use of heaters) influence others. Finally, the tutor reiterates the underlying theoretical concepts involved.

Figure 2.1 provides an example of typical student findings. It shows the variation in the humidity in a student's bathroom over a two-day period – the late night peaks in humidity levels allow for speculation about the student's bathing habits!

In summary, the experiential teaching and learning sequence employed is as follows:

1. concept formally introduced in lecture;

2. instructions for experiential practical given;

3. 'practical' carried out (learner gathers information in familiar environment);

4. data processed and results observed;

5. reflection on findings, followed by discussions;

6. concept and theory further reinforced.

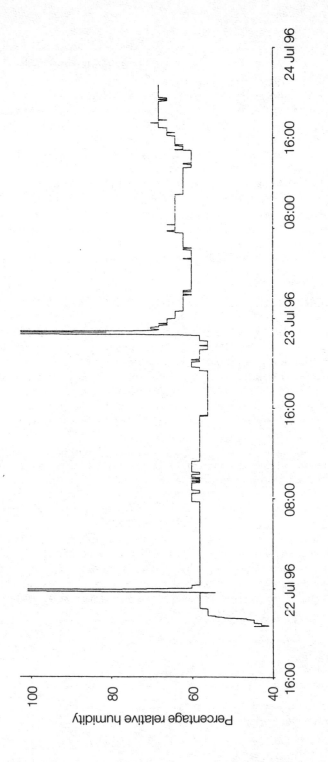

Figure 2.1 *An example of the use of a graph to illustrate results*

Ownership

All experimental work provides new data; this lends itself to ownership. In addition, the findings from experiential practicals are unique because of inevitable local and seasonal variations in environmental conditions. This uniqueness tends to increase interest and motivation, enhancing curiosity in the information and maximizing the feelings of ownership. Some students become anxious about the data validity. They are reassured that, provided the appropriate procedures were used, there is no reason to doubt the reliability and 'correctness' of their findings.

The data obtained helps students in appreciating enormous local variations in conditions – in the artificial, idealized world of the laboratory the aim is always to produce reproducible information. On the other hand, experiential practicals provide information in the absence of standardized laboratory conditions. Although this work is not scientific in the normal sense, trends and variations are nevertheless explainable by the underpinning sciences.

THE THEORETICAL PROCESSES RESULTING IN LEARNING

Our term *experiential practical* has been derived from experiential learning. The latter is defined by Long (1990) as '. . . that learning experience which arises from first of all undergoing a particular experience then, as a result of reflecting upon experience, extrapolating learning from it'. The experiences in an experiential practical are accumulated usually by merely being present (passively) in an environment for a reasonable length of time. Only when the environmental conditions reach extremes (eg too noisy, too cold, and too humid) does the individual actively experience the surroundings.

'Experiential learning does not mean that there is no input to the learners. What it does mean is that such input takes account of the experience of each learner and seeks to build upon that experience rather than being divorced from the reality experienced by the learner. It seeks to build a bridge between general truths/principles and the specific reality of the learner' (Long, 1990).

Experiential practicals attempt to bridge the gap between the theoretical, abstract (but required) ideas used in science teaching and the real world. It cannot be assumed that activity and experience alone directly cause learning. The feedback and reflection (as well as the teaching of the concepts) are critical for learning to take place. Indeed, the methodology allows the bulk of the students' time to be focused on analysis and interpretation rather than on manipulation of equipment.

EVALUATION

General comments

From our direct observations, there is no doubt that students are keen to participate and learn from the use of experiential practicals. Analysis of performance data, course evaluation forms and the use of questionnaires clearly shows that the students' learning experience and motivation are enhanced. The findings show that students obtain a better grasp of scientific concepts and a greater understanding of their relevance to the primary discipline. Certainly, the common phobia of disliking science appears to be almost non-existent in our courses.

Feedback obtained from marking the end of modules' examination questions also provides evidence that deep learning is taking place. Questions deliberately relate to real world circumstances, making it difficult to use cramming techniques during revision.

Examiners' comments

As the built environment field encompasses a number of disciplines, the science modules come under the scrutiny of at least six external examiners. While comments have generally been very favourable, several have consistently commented that the science examinations are difficult for first-year undergraduate level. Despite this, the average marks and pass rates compare very favourably with other level one subjects within the field. Although no formal comparative research has been carried out, we believe that the emphasis on the direct relevance of the subject by including experiential practicals is enormously beneficial.

CONCLUSION

The key lessons learnt from this work are:

- Much conventional teaching is often carried out in abstract, ie out of context, without examples and in the absence of direct involvement from students. For this reason, students frequently fail to appreciate the connection of theory with the real world. Thus certain core subjects are traditionally perceived as difficult and are unpopular. Where students can see the relevance and make the connections between theory and the real world, the level of interest and enthusiasm invariably improves.

- The teaching and learning method described in this chapter is derived from a mix of theoretical models of experiential learning and action research. The method emphasizes active learning and is designed to relate directly to the learners' practical life experiences and interests. This is especially useful when students have a diverse range of prior educational and employment histories.

- Experiential learning is that learning experience which arises from first undergoing a particular experience and then, as a result of reflecting upon experience, extrapolating learning from it. The input from the instructor takes account of and builds upon the experiences of each learner.

- Experiential practicals can take many forms but the key feature is that there is personal ownership of the unique data collected from familiar environments. The student makes interpretations and looks for trends; connections are inevitably made with the environment of experience and reasons for the variations are produced. This type of work is enormously beneficial in helping students to become familiar with new concepts.

- The gap between theoretical, abstract ideas and the real world experienced by the learner is bridged by experiential practicals, maximizing the relevant experience and learning. Activity, experience, feedback and reflection (as well as the teaching of the concepts) are critical for learning.

- Experiential practicals greatly enhance the students' learning experience, motivation and interest. Students obtain a better grasp of scientific concepts and a greater understanding of their relevance; there is ample evidence that deep learning is taking place. This method enhances curiosity, ensures student-centred learning and makes learning fun.

Acknowledgements

Extensive discussions with colleagues at conferences including the 4th International Improving Student Learning Symposium (Improving Student Learning Through Course Design), University of Bath (1996), The Encouraging Student Motivation Conference (SEDA), University of Plymouth (1997) and the 6th International Conference on Experiential Learning, Tampere (1998), have facilitated the development of the concepts which underpin experiential practicals.

REFERENCES

CIOB (1994) *Educational and Professional Development Manual*, The Chartered Institute of Building, Ascot, UK
HEFCE (1997) *Quality Assessment Report for the University of Luton in Building*, Higher Education Funding Council for England, Bristol
Long, DG (1990) *Learner Managed Learning*, Kogan Page, London
Mole, T (1997) *An Education and Training Framework for Chartered Building Surveyors*, The Royal Institution of Chartered Surveyors, London
Zuber-Skerritt, O (1992) *Action Research in Higher Education*, Kogan Page, London

3

Teaching Science to Non-science Students Using a Student-centred Classroom

Calvin S Kalman

SUMMARY

This chapter focuses on a physics-based course which is not available to engineering or science students and is not required for any degree programme or specifically for students' future employment.

Students, many from the fine arts, take it as an interest course or because some knowledge of science might be useful in the future. They have difficulty with computational methods and are not attuned to problem solving. The teaching uses the discipline-independent method of the student-centred classroom.

In addition to qualitative problems, this involves a variety of collaborative group and writing-to-learn methods. There are no formal examinations. Instead, students produce course dossiers. Students freewrite in their journals about material before the class, and also produce a critique based on the concepts they have come to understand after the week's classes. At the end of each semester, students develop an overview of the course with the assistance of two student reviewers. Students are also assigned to groups to study how a modern philosopher of science would view major topics in the course. Groups hand in a short summary of their findings and may be called on to make a short verbal presentation of the group's findings for the benefit of the entire class.

INTRODUCTION

The methodology used in the course has been tested in a number of courses using various experimental designs (Kalman, 1998; Kalman *et al*, 1999). Students have embraced the methods and have gone on to use them in other courses where such an approach is not required.

The institution

Concordia University is one of the largest urban universities in Canada. It is noted in the university's calendar that the institution 'has long promoted accessibility, innovation and an interdisciplinary approach to learning and its fundamental characteristics'. Concordia is a comprehensive university with roughly 14,000 full-time and 9,000 part-time students in faculties of arts and science, commerce, engineering and fine arts.

Students

The students are non-science students, who take courses where seminars are the norm. Many take fine arts programmes, some in philosophy and others in the science and human affairs programme. They are not used to using mathematics as a language for conceptual understanding and, indeed, are much more at ease with an essay-oriented approach. They are interested in having some understanding of science, but are nervous about the taking a course in this subject. The idea was to build a course that would be truly student centred, building on students' strengths in essay writing, employing group activities and utilizing writing-to-learn methodology (Kalman and Kalman, 1996, 1997, 1998).

Syllabus

The course surveyed all of science, emphasizing physics in particular, in two semesters. Students felt that the course would be of use in their subjects, but there was no requirement for them to take the subject. This in particular meant that they did not need to have any understanding of problem solving, which is usually a mainstay of such a course. Thus, assigned problems were almost entirely of a kind that emphasized conceptual understanding, rather than mathematical manipulation. Students were required to write about the material covered before and after each class. Additionally, each week they would hand in either a problem assignment or a group assignment. The problem and group assignments were generally alternated week by week. At the end of each semester, in lieu of an examination, they developed an overview. The sum of all their written work together constituted the course dossier. A summary of mark breakdown is as follows:

- assigned problems 20 per cent;
- group assignments 30 per cent;
- first semester dossier 25 per cent;
- second semester dossier 25 per cent.

Course objectives

These are:

- To understand how science functions. To this end, we will examine how three 20th century philosophers of science understand the scientific process – how theories evolve.

- To develop the critical thinking skills needed to critically analyse ideas and . compare them with observations of how nature functions. Students need to distinguish between concepts, hypotheses and observations of nature.

These are the actual course objectives found in the course outline handed out to all students. On the first and last days of the course, students are asked to write about the following question: 'In your view how does science work: how do theories come about and how do new theories take the place of older theories?' Based on this feedback, it is clear that students enter the course with what might be termed a Baconian outlook[1] on the function of science.

COLLABORATIVE GROUP WORK

Groups of three to five students are organized with the task of viewing course material through the eyes of a modern philosopher of science: Karl Popper, Thomas Kuhn or Imre Lakatos. The group work is seen as part of the overall attempt to get students to have a better understanding of science. For students to come to grips with the material, they must develop their critical thinking skills. They must come to understand and critically analyse their own views. Only then can they examine the evolution of science and develop ideas about how science works. The students present these ideas to the class and additionally hand in a written version. Only the written version is marked. To prevent piggy-backing, students hand in evaluation sheets with each assignment in which they rate the performance of each of the group members (see Appendix 3.1, page 24). In order that the rating not be seen as punitive, it is made clear that students will be given bonus marks for exceptional contributions. Normally students receive the mark actually given for the assignment. If any student is rated with a low participation for two consecutive assignments, the instructor takes this as a sign of a problem within the group and convenes a meeting with all group members to resolve any difficulties.

WRITING-TO-LEARN

Writing-to-learn helps students to learn how to learn and to apply what they learn, rather than memorizing what an expert has established. Additionally, writing-to-learn helps our students move to higher orders of thinking. By teaching writing-to-learn techniques, freewriting in particular, we help our students to write their way into an understanding of the course material and of their beliefs about that particular material.

Peter Elbow (1973) points out that writing is a recursive act, and can be viewed as a holistic process, involving successive drafts that move unevenly from an imprecise understanding of a text or problem through increasingly more complex, lucid and coherent interpretations. Through this process, which can take on many forms including the course dossier and freewrite-pair-share exercises, students can not only acquire new knowledge, but can come to change the preconceived concepts they enter university with, and which stand in the way of analytic and interpretive learning.

The course dossier

At Concordia, we use writing to ensure that students are aware of the concepts underlying the topics being discussed, rather than viewing the material as an agglomeration of disembodied facts and formulae to be learned. Students have to freewrite in their journals about material before the class with the result that a typical C student[2] is able to analyze material by developing questions and answering his or her own questions before the class. These students write their way into an understanding of difficult concepts, which they had not grasped before. Students produce a reflection before the class, based on the ideas they develop in the course of their freewritings and in addition, after the class, students write a critique based on the concepts the students have come to understand from the week's classes.

At the end of the semester, these students collect their critiques and write a single overview using the following procedure:

- First entries: two friends (student reviewers) read the material collected by the student and make comments.

- Second entries: the student rereads the critiques in conjunction with the comments and writes freely about it.

- Third entries: the second entries are used to develop some common theme(s) that run through the work.

- Fourth entries: the themes are developed into a draft of an overview.

- Fifth entries: the two friends read the draft and record their comments.

- Final entries: the draft is revised into an overview of the course. Suggested length three pages, but there is no page limit.

One student, who wrote a course dossier in the fall semester for an upper year regular physics course and began graduate work at another university in January, took time after leaving our physics department to write about his experience.[3] This student, who had just completed his final semester at Concordia with a grade point average (GPA) of 3.75[4], wrote that the course he had taken in his final semester 'is definitely one course that I will remember'. He valued the course not only for teaching him electromagnetic theory, but also because it 'taught me how to think'. He continues:

the post-summaries and the *post* post-summary [the course dossier] served two purposes. They allowed us to think on what had been presented in a critical manner and they made us translate our thoughts to paper in a clear manner. I believe that these two items can't be separated from each other. It doesn't matter how well one understands the material if one is not able to transmit the 'digested' ideas. I don't think that one could present ideas clearly without a thorough understanding of such ideas; so in a sense I think that the two items are really one.

Class meetings

As part of the development of the course dossier, students before each week's classes have prepared a reflection based on their readings of the material to be discussed that week. The instructor has prepared a series of transparencies covering various salient points. Students are led by the instructor into a discussion of the issues presented in these slides. To engage all the students in the activities, in many instances students are involved in freewrite-pair-share. In this case, students are asked to freewrite for a short fixed time on the material presented in the transparency and then share their conclusions with their neighbours. A general class discussion follows. In the process, students are led to realize that they carry preconceptions into the course. (In-depth analyses of student attitudes have been undertaken by McDermott 1984, McDermott *et al*, 1987; Halloun and Hestenes, 1985a, b; Gunstone, 1987; Rosenquist and McDermott, 1987; and Bowden *et al*, 1992). The basic conclusion is that students enter introductory courses with viewpoints differing significantly from the interpretation of how nature behaves that will be taught them and as they progress through the course these same students will go to great lengths to maintain this viewpoint. An interesting example concerns Galileo's development of the inertia concept. The class had a fair understanding of the idea that bodies would continue moving indefinitely in a horizontal path in the absence of frictional forces. After a class discussion, students were presented with the picture of a person in a balloon travelling upwards at five metres per second. The person drops a sandbag. Students were asked to perform a freewrite-pair-share exercise concerning the subsequent motion of the sandbag. After the class discussion, a vote was taken and it was found that almost all of the students believed that the sandbag would initially be at rest with respect to the ground. Students were then presented with a video that showed that their idea was contrary to the real situation. The real motion of the sandbag is related to the concept of inertia and the students came to realize that they had a preconception, which had not been changed by their readings. Their preconception had prevented them from translating their understanding of inertia related to horizontal motion to the vertical motion of the sandbag. This understanding of preconceptions was of great value to the students in understanding the difficulties faced by scientists in changing their theoretical outlooks.

CONCLUSION

The student-centred classroom involving qualitative problems, collaborative group and writing-to-learn methods and no formal examinations is a particularly effective method of teaching non-science students, who take courses where seminars are the norm. Group work assists students to achieve a better understanding of the evolution of science and to develop ideas about how science works. Writing-to-learn helps students to learn how to learn and to apply what they learn, rather than memorizing what an expert has established. Additionally, group work and writing-to-learn helps students move to higher orders of thinking. By teaching writing-to-learn techniques, freewriting in particular, we help students to write their way into an understanding of the course material and of their beliefs about that particular material.

The main points to note from the work presented in this chapter are:

- The methodology used in the course has been tested in a number of courses using various experimental designs.

- This is a truly student-centred course, building on the students strengths in essay writing, employing group activities and utilizing writing-to-learn methodology.

- In lieu of an examination, students develop a course dossier. This includes reflections before class, critiques after class and an overview developed with the assistance of two student reviewers.

- To engage all the students in the activities, in many instances during classes, students are involved in freewrite-pair-share.

- Groups of three to five students examine the course material through the eyes of a modern philosopher of science: Karl Popper, Thomas Kuhn or Imre Lakatos. The students present these ideas to the class and additionally hand in a written version.

Acknowledgements

Calvin Kalman credits his wife, Judy Kalman, who has had many successes in teaching writing at Concordia University, with inspiring much of his effort to bring writing into the science classroom. She also convinced him to set aside his initial scepticism of such writing methods as journalling to attend an intensive two-day workshop at the University of Vermont that encouraged him to try some new techniques himself.

NOTES

1. The philosophy of Francis Bacon dominated physics from the beginning of the 17th century to the end of the 19th century. The emphasis was on observation and induction: 'But my course and method . . . is not to extract

works from works or experiments from experiments, as an empiric, but from works and experiments to extract causes and axioms, and again from those causes and axioms new works and experiments, as a legitimate interpreter of nature'.

2.   The letter grade C commonly used in most North American universities corresponds to a mark of about 65 per cent.

3.   The student from Columbia would like his origin noted. He mentions that: 'If we are fortunate, people think of Columbia as a coffee producer, but most of the time the Columbia fame lies in drug trafficking'. Saying he is from Columbia 'will be a way of showing that Columbia is more than drugs and coffee'.

4.   Grade point averages (GPAs) are commonly calculated in North America to indicate the overall performance of students. A GPA of 3.75 on the scale of 0–4.3 represents an average mark of 80 per cent.

REFERENCES

Bowden, J *et al* (1992) Displacement, velocity, and frames of reference: Phenomeno-graphic studies of students' understanding and some implications for teaching and assessment, *American Journal of Physics*, **60**, pp 262–69

Elbow, P (1973) *Writing Without Teachers*, Oxford University Press, New York

Gunstone, RF (1987) Student understanding in mechanics: A large population survey, *American Journal of Physics*, **55**, pp 691–96

Halloun, IA and Hestenes, D (1985a) The initial knowledge of physics students, *American Journal of Physics*, **53**, pp 1043–55

Halloun, IA and Hestenes, D (1985b) Common sense concepts about motion, *American Journal of Physics*, **53**, pp 1056–65

Kalman, C *et al* (1999) Promoting conceptual change using collaborative groups in quantitative gateway courses, *American Journal of Physics*, Physics Educational Research Supplement

Kalman, J and Kalman, C (1996) Writing to learn, *American Journal of Physics*, **64**, pp 954–55

Kalman, J and Kalman, C (1997) Writing to learn, essays on teaching excellence 4, No 9, edited by Kay Herr Gillespie, The Professional and Organizational Development in Higher Education.

Kalman, C (1998) Developing critical thinking using cooperative learning techniques, *Physics in Canada*, January/February, pp 15–17

Kalman, J and Kalman, C (1998) Developing critical thinking using writing to learn techniques teaching learning connection, *Newsletter of the International Alliance of Teaching Scholars*, http://WWW.IATS.COM/Newsletter.html 1 (1)

McDermott, LC (1984), Research on conceptual understanding in mechanics, *Physics Today*, July, pp 24–32

McDermott, LC *et al* (1987) Student difficulties in connecting graphs and physics: Examples from kinematics, *American Journal of Physics*, **55**, pp 503–13

Rosenquist, ML and McDermott, LC (1987) A conceptual approach to teaching kine-matics, *American Journal of Physics*, **55**, pp 407–15

APPENDIX 3.1: PEER EVALUATION OF GROUP MEMBERS

Team

Purpose: To ensure that the 'team component' of each individual's grade reflects each person's contributions to the group project.

Assumption: When a member has contributed to the overall work of the team about the same as the average team member in total, he or she should receive 100 per cent of the 'overall team grade' for the team component of the course.

When a member has made exceptional contributions to the work of the team (eg analytical, organizational, written, investigative, verbal) he or she should receive a higher grade (eg 110 per cent, 120 per cent of the team grade).

Similarly, when a member has been contributing less than other members, he or she should receive a lower grade (eg 90 per cent, 80 per cent of the team grade).

There is no requirement that the overall percentage average 100 per cent. For example, it is possible for one member to receive 110 per cent and the rest of the group to receive 100 per cent.

Instructions: List below the members of your team and indicate what percentage of the team grade you recommend for yourself and for each other team member. If you have listed a percentage other than 100 per cent for any team member, please indicate underneath the evaluations or on back of the form an explanation for the evaluation. For example group member X did extra research, summarizing the material of a number of relevant chapters for the group.

Name   Percentage

1. Yourself _____

2. _____

3. _____

4. _____

5. _____

6. _____

4

Problem-based Learning

Peter Ommundsen

SUMMARY

The author shows how problem-based learning can be used to overcome the problems which arise when students are required to take a core subject (he uses the example of biology) for which they fail to perceive a relevance to their chosen careers.

Problem-based learning (PBL) inspires students by involving them in meaningful activities rather than requiring them to listen passively to lectures. Students are presented with interesting case problems to solve, and the students learn the subject by discussing and investigating the problems in small groups.

PBL is adaptable to a lecture theatre environment, where the instructor acts as a facilitator, circulating among the small groups. PBL students learn the subject while developing skills as self-directed learners.

Research literature supports the efficacy of PBL as a means of inspiring students.

INTRODUCTION

Biology is a core subject for many career paths, including forestry, pharmacy, psychology, education, physiotherapy, and medicine. However, students may not be inspired by traditional biology syllabi, which often prescribe mindless memorization.

A better educational environment can be created by employing problem-based learning (PBL), which engages students in solving intriguing and bizarre case problems in cooperative groups. Problem-based learning emulates the workplace, captures student interest, and develops self-directed learners.

STUDENT POPULATION

Selkirk College is a Canadian community college with a mission of improving access to education, and consequently attracts a diverse student population.

The institution is tax-supported, fees are relatively low, and admission is by order of application rather than by academic rank.

Students within a biology course vary in age, background experience, career goal, and academic ability. A typical beginning first year biology class of 70 students has an average score of 66 per cent (range 45–100) on the Analytical Skills Inventory, a diagnostic test of verbal skills and reasoning ability (Whimbey and Lochhead, 1986). Many students do not initially perceive the relevance of basic science to their future studies, and this creates a challenge for instructors.

METHOD

The introductory biology course includes three 50-minute periods per week of class meeting time and one three-hour laboratory. In a PBL course, class meeting time is used to occupy students with active learning, although PBL need not entirely replace lectures. Students form small groups within the lecture theatre and are given an open-ended, authentic case problem that is likely to pique their interest in biology. Occasionally a video clip or specimen might be used as a trigger. A typical case presentation states: 'A 94-year-old woman admitted to hospital with pneumonia had an enlarged abdomen. A scan of her abdomen revealed the presence of a foetus. The woman had dementia and so was unable to explain what had happened'.

The instructor challenges the students to solve the problem – to explain an apparent pregnancy in a 94-year-old woman. The students are eager to do so because they are solving a mystery. Students take the initiative to learn about the biology of reproduction, working in small groups to generate possible solutions, and may consult their text, course manual, and instructor. The students thus take ownership of the agenda and define the learning issues, while the instructor functions as a resource and facilitator. Learning is reinforced by students themselves, discussing the biology within their small groups. If a case problem extends beyond a single class session, students might refer to the library or Internet.

During the class, the instructor may selectively release further information about the case in response to thoughtful questions, and the instructor may assist in explaining biological concepts, individually or via brief lectures. Students are keen to hear such lectures, as they are in service of their immediate learning needs. The extent to which the instructor provides such assistance depends upon the ability of the students and the stage of the course. Ideally, student-directed learning should be maximized.

The instructor eventually asks that a representative from each group write a solution on the board. The instructor then reconvenes the entire class and leads a discussion regarding the proposals. This session provides feedback, elaborates the biology, and reveals details that should enable student groups to completely resolve the problem. Finally, the instructor may ask that the students submit a short written report that incorporates the biology used to illuminate the case.

In a PBL classroom, learning is problem driven. Students perceive learning as relevant because it is in service of completing a task, solving a problem. Learning occurs on a need-to-know basis, as in a workplace. It is the students who control the agenda. The role of the instructor is to craft a spectrum of problems that involves students with the important concepts of biology. In a PBL classroom instruction begins with a problem. This differs from a traditional classroom, in which instruction begins with a lecture, and students may be unaware of its application in a meaningful context.

PBL students assimilate factual knowledge, but they also discover how to analyze problems, how to retrieve information, and how to become self-directed learners. In contrast, students of a lecture-based classroom may simply watch, memorize, and repeat what they have been told.

SAMPLE CASE PROBLEM

PBL begins on the first day of the course and provides an appealing introduction to the subject. The following example illustrates the sequence of events that occurs during the class session.

Small group formation

During the initial class meeting of the course, some 70 students are gathered in a lecture theatre. The instructor provides a brief description of PBL, group skills, and a problem-solving heuristic. Students then form groups of three to five people by lottery or by choice of partners.

Problem presentation

The instructor presents the following problem, emphasizing that it is an authentic problem from a real-life case history: 'A 58-year-old woman was admitted to hospital because of recurrent episodes of confusion. She occasionally experienced hazy vision, could not concentrate, and might repeat what she was saying as many as 30 times'. Prior to class the instructor has reviewed the case history (Scully *et al*, 1988; see also Service, 1995) and has selected data to release incrementally as the case proceeds. The launch of the problem energizes the learning environment, especially if accompanied by instructor enthusiasm and theatricality.

Activation of groups

The student groups are allotted 15 minutes to brainstorm possible solutions, to discuss these among themselves, and to write their top priority hypothesis on the blackboard. A typical list produced by the students might include stroke, alcoholism, dementia, epilepsy, drug abuse, Alzheimer's disease, meningitis, atherosclerosis, cancer, emphysema, diabetes, and trauma.

The fact that the students can produce such a list on the first day of the course sends them several messages:

- students themselves are instructional resources and they can learn from each other; they are capable of self-directed learning;
- they are capable of tackling a problem.

This last point is important for problem-wary students who have arrived from a mimetic educational background.

Provision of feedback

The instructor reconvenes the class as a whole and congratulates the students on their work. The instructor elicits discussion on the biological justification for each of the hypotheses that the students placed on the board, and solicits questions about the case from the students. Student questions may probe possible relationships among variables: 'When did the attacks of confusion occur? Following a drinking episode?'

When informed that the attacks usually occurred in the late afternoon, the students will likely raise questions regarding diet and blood sugar. At this point the instructor can focus attention on the biology of carbohydrates and the regulation of blood sugar, using a transparency, a copy of which each student has in the course manual. Next, students may ask for data on sugar levels in the blood (low) and urine (zero) of the woman. A student worksheet (see Appendix 4.1) facilitates an orderly approach to problem solving.

The cycle of small group work and instructor feedback can be continued during the current class session or on future occasions. Student groups can investigate causes of low blood sugar, and may suggest anorexia nervosa, extreme exercise, insulin-poisoning, glucagon-deficiency, adrenal failure, etc. Problem-focused students are anxious to fully understand biological mechanisms, so learning is of greater depth than superficial memorization of facts. The instructor circulates among student groups, providing assistance, but not solutions. Groups may well explore avenues unanticipated by the instructor. This is highly desirable and should not be discouraged. The instructor should avoid controlling the agenda of the groups.

Newly generated hypotheses can be placed on the chalkboard as before, and further feedback given by the instructor. The class will likely request an X-ray image of the woman's abdomen, as the pancreas is important in blood sugar regulation. The abdominal scan provides a good anatomy lesson, as the students must identify the various organs. Additional images may include ultrasonograms, angiograms, and microscopic anatomy. Each offers new learning opportunities. In this case an insulin-secreting tumour is present in the pancreas.

Submission of a report

The student groups are now asked to write a report that employs their knowledge of the biology of the case.

FURTHER EXAMPLES OF CASE PROBLEMS SUITABLE FOR GENERAL BIOLOGY

Effective case problems are open-ended, allowing students to investigate many facets of biology. Although the goal of the student is to solve a problem, the goal of the instructor is to teach biology. It is thus desirable to prolong the resolution of the problem in order to maximize the amount of biology that students must explore.

Case problems are easily culled from the literature by the instructor. Needless to say, students should not be given the citations, as the goal of PBL is to solve problems, not read solutions.

Simple problem statements, such as the following, are sufficient to activate student groups:

- A 30-year-old woman squeezing the toothpaste was unable to release her grip.

- A 24-year-old man experienced abdominal pain whenever he consumed sugar.

- A forest patch was logged, then replanted, but within seven years the newly planted trees began to die.

- A woman with type O blood gave birth to a child with blood type AB.

- A 28-year-old man developed osteoporosis.

- A population of rare marmots has declined by 60 per cent in the past 10 years.

- An 80-year-old woman suffered from confusion and falls. Her lungs were gritty like hard sponges.

- A farmer noticed that some crop plants wilted badly and could only be grown in a greenhouse.

- An 88-year old man consumed 25 eggs per day for many years, yet had a normal blood cholesterol level.

- A 47-year-old woman had for eight years experienced sweating and flushing. Her pulse ranged from 76 to 120 and her blood pressure was 170/139.

- Fish returning to a salmon-spawning river produced a small fraction of the expected number of eggs.

- A 23-year-old body builder had large muscles but his testes were half normal size.

- An outbreak of illness (121 cases) was characterized by sleeplessness, headache, shortness of breath, rapid heart rate, sweating, tremors, heat intolerance, and weight loss.

- A fitness test of fire-fighter applicants resulted in 32 hospitalizations with back pain, muscle pain, and reduced urine output. One applicant died.

- Four hundred young women at a rock concert collapsed or experienced faintness as a result of six different causes.

- A 61-year-old man suffered from garbled speech, but only while talking on the telephone.

- A nine-year-old boy had experienced recurrent infections of the chest, ears, and sinuses for a period of eight years.

- Why is this plant abnormal? (The instructor can grow plants with hormonal or microbial pathologies; these can be researched further by the students in investigative laboratories.)

- Suspects in a murder trial are linked to certain evidence by DNA-typing (simulated criminal trial using real forensic laboratory DNA autorads).

The PBL format also is well suited to developing skills of critical thinking and bioethical analysis. Student groups can critique claims of local alternative health practitioners (Angell and Kassirer, 1998) and dissect bioethical dilemmas (Fackelmann, 1994).

EVALUATION

Does PBL inspire students? Is an instructor justified in adopting PBL to complement or replace conventional teaching? Certainly the adoption of PBL seems justified by student enthusiasm and by favourable comments on course evaluation questionnaires. However, the decision to use PBL also is grounded in educational research.

Experience with PBL has been gained in many disciplines, including basic science, health science, economics, engineering, law, and social work, to name a few (Boud and Feletti, 1991). PBL techniques vary (Barrows, 1986), so caution is required in treating PBL as a single independent variable. Nevertheless, a number of studies have suggested a positive effect of PBL when compared to conventional courses. PBL has been shown to improve class attendance, improve student library use, improve attitudes, and improve analytic skills (Vernon and Blake, 1993; Dolmans and Schmidt, 1996; Kaufman and Mann, 1997). Future research may identify the relative contribution of each component of the PBL experience.

CONCLUSION

A problem-based learning environment inspires students by involving them in solving biological case problems:

- Instruction begins with presentation of a problem.

- Problems are authentic, and are chosen to capture student interest.

- Problems are open-ended, allowing exploration of many facets of biology.

- Learning is problem driven. Students learn by experience while seeking and applying knowledge towards resolution of the problem.

- The classroom emulates the workplace, in which people undertake meaningful tasks.

- Learning is active rather than passive.

- Student interaction shapes behaviour and forms a stimulus-rich learning field. Students receive immediate reinforcement via group discussion and instructor feedback.

- Learning is student-directed. Students themselves identify the learning issues, while the instructor acts as a facilitator.

REFERENCES

Angell, M and Kassirer, JP (1998) Alternative medicine: The risks of untested and unregulated remedies, *The New England Journal of Medicine*, **339**, pp 839–41

Barrows, HS (1986) A taxonomy of problem-based learning methods, *Medical Education*, **20**, pp 481–86

Boud, D and Feletti, G (eds) (1991) *The Challenge of Problem Based Learning*, Kogan Page, London

Dolmans, D and Schmidt, H (1996) The advantages of problem-based curricula, *The Postgraduate Medical Journal*, **72**, pp 535–58

Fackelmann, KA (1994) DNA dilemmas: Readers and experts weigh in on biomedical ethics, *Science News*, **146**, pp 408–10

Kaufman, DM and Mann, KV (1997) Basic sciences in problem-based learning and conventional curricula: Students' attitudes, *Medical Education*, **31**, pp 177–80

Scully, RE et al (1988) Case records of the Massachusetts General Hospital, case 23–1988, *The New England Journal of Medicine*, **318**, pp 1523–32

Service, FJ (1995) Hypoglycemic disorders, *The New England Journal of Medicine*, **332**, pp 1144–52

Vernon, DTA and Blake, RL (1993) Does problem-based learning work? A meta-analysis of evaluative research, *Academic Medicine*, **68**, pp 550–63

Whimbey, A and Lochhead, J (1986) *Problem Solving and Comprehension*, Lawrence Erlbaum Associates, New Jersey

APPENDIX 4.1 EXAMPLE OF STUDENT WORKSHEET

A CASE OF CONFUSION

BACKGROUND

A 58-year-old woman was admitted to hospital because of recurrent episodes of confusion. She occasionally experienced hazy vision, could not concentrate, and might repeat what she was saying as many as 30 times.

How to make a DENT in a problem: Define, Explore, Narrow, Test.

1. DEFINE the question carefully: What are you trying to find out? What caused episodes of confusion in a 58-year-old woman?
2. EXPLORE possible solutions.
3. NARROW your choices: weed, sort, prioritize.
4. TEST your ideas: obtain further information.

List these below:

Alzheimer's Disease	1	Memory test normal
Alcoholism	2	No evidence of alcohol abuse
Low blood pressure	3	Blood pressure = 160/95
Low blood glucose	4	Low glucose: 1.6 mmol/L
Emphysema	6	Normal X-ray film, no dyspnea
Heart rhythm abnormality	8	Electrocardiogram normal
Low blood calcium	7	Calcium normal, 2.43 mmol/L
Diabetes mellitis	5	No glucose in urine

CONCLUSION

This woman was found to have an insulin-secreting tumour in her pancreas, causing her brain to be deprived of glucose, and resulting in episodes of confusion. Glucose is a fuel used by the brain and other organs. Insulin is a hormone secreted by beta cells in the pancreatic islets. Insulin assists the uptake of glucose from the blood by muscle and fat cells. Insulin also inhibits the release of glucose from the liver into the bloodstream. When excess insulin is present, the level of glucose in the blood will become very low, inadequate for normal brain function. In this woman the blood glucose level was only 1.6 mmol/L. A normal blood glucose level is approximately 3.9–6.1 mmol/L. Behavioural changes may occur when the blood glucose level falls to about 1.9 mmol/L.

5

Enhancing Motivation and Learning Through Collaboration and the Use of Problems

John R Savery

SUMMARY

Instructors of required courses in any discipline often encounter students who appear less motivated to learn. These students must pass the required courses regardless of their current knowledge or skill in the subject domain, or their level of interest in the course content, and consequently student interest may be lacking.

This chapter reports on the exemplary work of two instructors who re-designed their 'required' course to increase student motivation while maintaining a focus on essential skills and knowledge. The course was delivered through a combination of:

- instructional simulation;
- collaborative learning;
- use of authentic problems;
- effective mentoring;
- effective team teaching.

This chapter describes how the two instructors were able to inspire and instruct over 200 students each semester.

INTRODUCTION

This semester-long case study was set in an undergraduate course in the school of business of a large, mid-western university, in the United States. Since all business school undergraduates were required to take a business communications course, regardless of their particular area of interest (finance, real estate, accounting, etc), or prior accomplishments in any other English courses, the range of interest in the subject, and levels of prior knowledge varied greatly. The two full-time instructors who participated in the study, Anna Weston and Judy McCloud, had used a traditional lecture/laboratory approach to teach this course for the past 17 years. However, as McCloud said, 'There had to be a better way to teach writing, than talking about writing'. Concurrently, within the school of business, there was a concern with the inability of undergraduate students to demonstrate effective problem-solving skills. Thus, Weston and McCloud were supported in their efforts to redesign their business communications course to foster problem-solving skills with the expectation that students would still master traditional course objectives. The teachers spent several months designing the course and developing materials before actually implementing the revised course with students.

METHODS AND SUBJECTS

The instructors team-taught four sections with 50 students per section. These 200 students were organized into five-person teams that met twice per week for 75 minute class sessions. All classes were held in two adjoining computer laboratories. One volunteer team from each class was selected based on their willingness to participate, their group composition, and the computer laboratory in which they were physically present for the semester. Of the 20 second-year students volunteering for this study, 14 were male and six were female. Three teams had two female students and three male students, while the fourth team had five male students. Nineteen students were Caucasian and one was African-American. This sample was representative of the larger student population. All 20 students passed the course and each of the four teams remained intact for the complete semester.

Designing a course to enhance motivation was one aspect of a multiple case study (Savery, 1996) that examined issues of student ownership for learning. This multiple-case study (guidelines by Yin, 1992) used the following data collection methods:

- participant observation of each team for 26 class sessions;

- documentation including forms completed by students, teacher-developed writing scenarios, quizzes, and course grading sheets for individuals and teams;

- multiple student rating surveys;

- interviews with each student at mid-course and during the final week of class;

- two structured interviews with each teacher;

- in-class videotaping of each team during four consecutive classes (a complete project cycle).

These data collection strategies provided multiple perspectives on the learning experiences of individual students, student teams and the course instructors.

DESIGN OF THE COURSE AND LEARNING ENVIRONMENT

Weston and McCloud were contributing authors to textbooks on business communication as well as consultants and instructors in the corporate environment. Based on their rich knowledge of writing in the world of business, they designed a simulation of a multinational corporation to provide their students with a business context for the writing assignments, and an organizational framework for the course. During the first class meeting, they explained how the course would be run like a business and how business criteria for effective correspondence would be used consistently. Students received a detailed 'Employee Handbook' (which effectively functioned as the course syllabus) containing a history of the corporation, the organizational structure, clearly stated expectations for all employees (course objectives) as well as the policies and procedures to be followed by all employees. The instructors stated very clearly that there would be no lectures, that each student was expected to be mature, responsible and self-directed in their learning, and that much of their grade depended on collaborative teamwork. Any students who felt they lacked the maturity to be responsible learners, or felt uncomfortable with the collaborative team approach were encouraged to transfer to a lecture-based section of the course as soon as possible.

As new employees, the students received training on the tools (software applications) to be used in their new jobs. Students with acceptable skill levels could sign a waiver and skip the training sessions. Students also completed an inventory in which they rated their current skills and knowledge on a range of technical and interpersonal items. Using these inventories, the teachers assigned students to five-person teams with a mix of skills, and provided a non-graded training unit to help the teams develop their collaboration skills. Over the remaining 12 weeks of the semester, the teams rotated through four, two-week long departments (human resources, marketing, accounting, and purchasing) and one, four-week long department (operations) where they were presented with complex problem scenarios that required a written response. The teams worked collaboratively to produce the best possible written solution to each problem situation. Over two weeks (four class sessions) the teams analysed the problems, determined an appropriate response, and produced a final written product printed on company letterhead.

Both teachers were familiar with the different writing assignments, but coached and graded separately to ensure consistency between teams and classes. Thus, Weston was the teacher/coach, resource person and evaluator for all student teams working in the purchasing and human resources departments, while McCloud fulfilled the same responsibilities for teams in the marketing and accounting departments. The primary teacher resource for each team was determined by the departmental rotation, not the room assignment. Teachers moved constantly between the adjoining computer laboratories to help the teams that had rotated into their departmental responsibility area. In contrast, when a team rotated into the operations department, the teacher in their assigned home laboratory became their mentor for that assignment and also the person to whom they presented their written and oral reports.

Weston and McCloud had taught their alternative course four times prior to this study and were well prepared with multiple sets of problem situations for each department. New problem situations drawn from articles in business journals/newspapers were added each semester and problem situations from previous semesters were modified to increase or decrease the level of difficulty based on past student performance. For example, the team in the human resources department might receive this problem:

> As Human Resources Manager, you have interviewed William Sears and Alicia Stewart, two applicants for the same position. It's a difficult decision because both candidates impressed you.
>
> You decide to offer the job to Alicia because her work experience more nearly matches the requirements of the job. Write a letter to Alicia offering her the job. Be sure to identify the position, the salary, and the starting date.
>
> In addition, you want to send a tactful letter to the other applicant, William. While William didn't have quite the right experience for this job, you were impressed with his energy and motivation. There are no other openings at the company right now, but you may want to hire him for another position in the future. Write a letter explaining to William that he didn't get the job.

The longer operations department problem usually involved the students in the preparation of a detailed report based on research. For example:

> Starr Property Management is opening a department store in Xyz. Approximately 10 employees will transfer there to manage the department store, and they will be working side-by-side with many local skilled professionals. You realize that working in a culturally diverse environment can be filled with communication problems. The communication problems often have as much to do with cultural norms and expectations as with language. In addition, inappropriate nonverbal messages can cloud communication by confusing, embarrassing, or offending others. The amount of eye contact, type of hand gestures, and levels of formality your employees use when communicating can positively or negatively affect the results they achieve.
>
> You want to be sure your employees recognize that people from other cultures may think differently, act differently, learn differently, and write differently. Your employees must be trained in cultural etiquette to work successfully with the local employees so that their behaviour and attitudes will be appropriate. Prepare a written report to help these employees work successfully in their new setting.
>
> Investigate topics such as the following:

- differences in behaviour, protocol, etiquette;
- informality/formality in business, business practices;
- women's roles;
- food, drink, money, interpersonal relations;
- leadership behaviours.

The written report should include a title page, memo of transmittal, contents, list of illustrations, executive summary, body (introduction, discussion, conclusion), and works cited.

Plan a 30-minute oral presentation for Starr Property Management employees (a group of young adults) who are being transferred. The purpose of this presentation is to gather the employees in one location, to present each employee with a copy of the written report (only one report is necessary), and to present additional information.

The 30-minute oral presentation could summarize the written report, emphasize the most important material and present new information. After listening to the oral presentation and reading the written report, the employees should feel confident and ready for their transfer. You will want to make the presentation interesting. Be sure to include computer graphics in your presentation.

Regardless of the department, student teams would encounter variations on the four basic types of letter writing situations: good news, bad news, persuasive, and routine. A typical problem situation would include background information about the problem and specific information to guide the writing process. The teachers planned for student teams to become expert with the four most frequently used types of business correspondence by providing multiple examples in significantly different contexts. Individual students were expected to learn each of the four letter types by authoring or co-authoring at least one of each type, and by reviewing or critiquing the work of teammates. However, selection of individual writing assignments was determined within the teams. The more self-directed learners often chose different writing situations to expand their understanding of all the letter types; the other team members often chose to repeat a letter type in the hope of improving their grade or expending less effort.

Team members shared the grade for group work and were expected to participate fully to ensure that the best quality of writing was produced. The 60 per cent of the individual grade based on group work was balanced by 40 per cent for individual scores, earned through peer evaluations (15 per cent), attendance (10 per cent), examinations (10 per cent), and article summaries (5 per cent). Students completed three confidential peer evaluations over the semester. The teachers tabulated the scores and informed students with very high scores or very low scores of their peer approval rating. The final exam was a timed writing situation similar to tasks set earlier in the course, but weighted more heavily. The article summary task required students to read a business related newspaper or journal article (supplied), write a concise summary, and send it via electronic mail to the teacher.

Students were encouraged to treat the computer laboratory as their office and act as they would in a work environment. Teams typically found an area in the laboratory that became their work area. As in most work environments, there was time for socializing and students often talked about relationships with boyfriends or girlfriends, holiday plans, sports events, recent adventures, other courses, and a multitude of other topics. The learning environment was relaxed, and, except during individualized testing (spot quizzes), there was a constant hum of multiple conversations (both on and off-task), that was pleasant and never disruptive. Students effectively tuned-out extraneous noise to concentrate on the writing assignments, and used their time in the computer laboratory efficiently. Those students with full course loads and part-time jobs loudly expressed their appreciation at being able to complete their writing assignments during class time. Attendance by the 20 students in the sample was high (90 per cent). Most teams stayed on-task during class to complete assignments and also encouraged the less well-organized members of their team to do the same. This produced more on-task behaviours, better use of available resources (teacher, textbooks, resource books), discussion between team members, and helping behaviours.

INSTRUCTIONAL SCAFFOLDING AND COACHING

For the first writing project Weston and McCloud provided extensive coaching and occasionally direct instruction. When the teachers met with a team, students asked questions that revealed their thinking about the problem. Within the context of the specific problem, the teachers provided both cognitive structuring and global questioning strategies. These included the heuristics of effective writers such as:

- What is your primary purpose?

- What is your secondary purpose?

- Who is your audience/reader?

- What do they need to do with this information?

- Is the direct or indirect approach appropriate in this situation?

As Mary, in the 9.30 am team put it: 'I think the teachers want us to learn on our own and in our group before we come to her and ask, "How do I do this?" She'll give us a few hints and pushes in the right direction, which is good [but] she doesn't just sit down and explain how to do everything'.

Weston and McCloud frankly admitted that moving between groups and responding to context-specific questions could be very challenging. However, they both found this format more rewarding than responding to the same questions asked repeatedly by students in a large class working on the same assignment. The 5 to 10 minutes per class that a teacher spent with an individual team was highly focused and contextualized. Consequently, students were provided with an appropriate level of assistance as they progressed from novice to more expert writers.

Both instructors believed that it was very important that students develop teacher independence and self-directed learning skills. As the semester progressed, they encouraged students to use their teammates as the primary source of information and assistance. Student reaction to this transfer of responsibility for learning was mixed. Students with a high degree of teacher dependency were resentful and tried many different tactics to get the teacher to answer their questions; or confirm that they 'had it right'. Students on teams where there was minimal collaboration continued to seek teacher guidance and support. Students that were more self-directed in their learning or members of collaborative teams adapted to the reduction in teacher support with little or no difficulty. As Sam, a member of the 11.15 am team said:

> . . . I think with this class it's more of a self-struggle to learn because we're not getting lectured to . . . we have to read the book ourselves, we have to read the examples ourselves, we have to synthesise the letters ourselves. We have to read and we have to prepare and we have to know what we are doing. It's more of a struggle, it's not that hard but . . . if you want to learn anything you've got to do it yourself. You can't expect to go to class, get notes and just read those notes. You have to do it yourself so I think it's very, very focused on me and my learning how to do these things.

Sam was exceptionally articulate but also representative of the majority of the students in the study group.

Although it was not directly apparent to the students, this learning environment was well planned, and highly structured, particularly in the design and implementation of projects (Blumenfeld *et al*, 1991; Cohen, 1994) that were both challenging and motivating. It reflected the teachers stated intention of helping students to become more independent, responsible and self-directed, or as Weston described it: 'Doing their own reading, own thinking and not always asking the teacher for answers'. The intended learning outcomes, (a) effective business writing, (b) effectively collaborative teamwork, and (c) effective use of computer applications, were realized through the organization of the course content and the design of the learning environment.

ANALYSIS

Although Weston and McCloud had no formal training in the design of instructional simulations, and they had never heard of 'constructivism' as a learning theory/instructional approach, they intuitively used authentic problems whenever possible. Their approach encouraged the social negotiation of meaning by student teams, and built interdependence into the collaborative learning tasks. They provided all students with an opportunity to master the important aspects of the course content, develop skills and self-confidence in their ability to apply those skills to novel problem situations and inspired many students to become leaders in their groups. It was apparent the teachers used a cognitive apprenticeship approach (Collins, Brown, and Newman, 1989) and recognized the importance of the social milieu (Gallimore and Tharp, 1990; Rogoff, 1990, 1994; Vygotsky, 1978) within which learning occurred and its significant influence on what was learned. The teachers' efforts to develop a learning community where ideas are discussed and understanding enriched was a critical component in the design of this effective learning environment (Brown and Palinscar, 1989; Rogoff, 1990).

Perhaps most importantly, the teachers expected (and trusted) that given the opportunity, students would become self-directed and self-managing with respect to task completion and quality standards. It is apparent that the teachers viewed learners as metacognitively, motivationally, and behaviourally proactive participants in their own learning process (Zimmerman and Schunk, 1989).

Increasing student motivation to learn was an important element in the design of this required course. Several authors (Brooks and Brooks, 1993; Savery and Duffy, 1995; Duffy and Cunningham, 1996) have suggested that the design of effective learning communities may be fostered by the application of specific instructional principles and there was evidence that in this alternative format that teachers:

- anchored all learning activities to a larger task or problem;

- designed an authentic task such that the task and the learning environment reflected the complexity of the environment students should be able to function in after instruction;

- gave the learner ownership of the process used to develop a solution and supported the learner in developing ownership for the overall problem or task;

- supported and challenged the learner's thinking while encouraging the testing of ideas against alternative views and alternative contexts;

- provided learners with an opportunity and support for reflection on both the content learned and the learning process.

CONCLUSIONS

It was apparent that the majority of these undergraduate students flourished in this learner-centred environment and demonstrated increased motivation and mastery in the course content. Many students commented that they appreciated being treated as responsible adults, encouraged to articulate their writing situations, collaborate with a peer, share their knowledge, and negotiate a meaningful response to the problem situations. They further commented that the course had significantly less busy work than most courses, provided focused mentoring by an experienced expert in the field, and provided an environment that rewarded the efficient use of class time.

By continually adapting and modifying their instructional efforts, these teachers have designed a learning environment that is rich in complexity and authentic learning opportunities. This course set out to develop a set of skills and knowledge related to the writing of properly formatted, concise, clear, and effective business communications, and to increase the level of self-directed learning, self-regulation, and teacher independence of these undergraduate students. Through the design of this learner-centred instructional environment, the teachers were able to improve the writing skills of the study participants while simultaneously enhancing the self-regulated learning skills of all students on their course.

REFERENCES

Blumenfeld, PC *et al* (1991) Motivating project-based learning: Sustaining the doing, supporting the learning, *Educational Psychologist*, **26** (3/4), pp 369–98

Brooks, JG and Brooks, MG (1993) *In Search of Understanding: The case for constructivist classrooms*, Association for Supervision and Curriculum Development, Alexandria, VA

Brown, AL and Palinscar, AS (1989) Guided cooperative learning and individual knowledge acquisition, in *Cognition and Instruction: Issues and agendas*, ed L Resnick, Erlbaum, Hillsdale, NJ

Cohen, E (1994) Restructuring the classroom: Conditions for productive small groups, Review of *Educational Research*, **64**, pp 1–35

Collins, A, Brown, JS, and Newman, SE (1989) Cognitive apprenticeship: Teaching the crafts of reading, writing and mathematics, in *Knowing, Learning and Instruction: Essays in honor of Robert Glaser*, ed L Resnick, Erlbaum, Hillsdale NJ

Duffy, TM and Cunningham, DJ (1996) Constructivism: Implications for the design and delivery of instruction, in *Handbook of Instructional Technology*, ed D Jonassen, Macmillan, New York

Gallimore, R and Tharp, R (1990) Teaching mind in society: Teaching, schooling and literate discourse, in *Vygotsky and Education*, ed LC Moll, Cambridge University Press, Cambridge

Rogoff, B (1990) *Apprenticeship in Thinking: Cognitive development in social context*, Oxford University Press, New York

Rogoff, B (1994) Developing understanding of the idea of communities of learners, *Mind, Culture and Activity*, **1**, pp 209–29

Savery, JR (1996) Fostering student ownership for learning in a learner centered instructional environment, doctoral dissertation, Indiana University, Bloomington IN

Savery, JR and Duffy, TM (1995) Problem-based learning: An instructional model and its constructivist framework, *Educational Technology*, **35** (5), pp 31–38

Vygotsky, LS (1978) *Mind in Society: The development of higher psychological processes*, Harvard University Press, Cambridge, MA

Yin, R (1992) *Case Study Research: Designs and Methods*, Sage Publications, London

Zimmerman, BJ and Schunk, DH (1989) *Self-regulated Learning and Academic Achievement: Theory, research and practice*, Springer-Verlag, New York

6

Simulation in Management Education

Mark W Teale

SUMMARY

This chapter reviews a change of teaching a particular unit within a UK school of business. The original delivery was through traditional lectures and seminars. The new approach places more emphasis on experiential learning and mentoring; this has resulted in increased student enjoyment.

The chapter describes the development of the unit and the philosophy behind the components, how these were produced and the operation of the unit in practice.

An aim of the new unit is to encourage students to learn more effectively by developing their own learning skills. The unit simulates the decision-making process and includes a model that generates the effects of decisions taken. The unit requires students to learn in a small group environment, where they help each other achieve the learning outcomes. The unit is based on established learning theories.

The impetus for the redesign came partly from recognition of resource constraints on teaching, but mainly from the author's interest in questioning the students' learning processes.

INTRODUCTION

This case study describes how teaching is evolving within the operations management interest group at the University of Lincolnshire and Humberside (ULH). The development began in 1994 and the first delivery was in 1995/96. The concept has been applied to intermediate undergraduate programmes as well as Master's programmes locally and internationally. The performance of the unit is assessed through student and tutor feedback, which indicates performance and learning benefits. The principal objective of the new style of delivery was to enhance the learning experience of the students. The subject of operations management is difficult for many undergraduate students to relate to, especially if they have little work experience.

Student profile

ULH provides students with the opportunity to follow a modular path resulting in named awards, such as business and finance. Operations management is a compulsory module on the second-year business major, and forms part of other named awards, including substantial contributions to a variety of Master's programmes. The number of students studying operations management, in one form or another, in 1995/96 was more than 1500 per annum across a number of campuses. An optional unit at intermediate level that typically had a cohort of 120 students was the focus for the development. A mix of students, local, international and mature, with a variety of educational backgrounds, take the unit. Knowledge of, or acquaintance with, operations management is normally the exception.

Knowledge of operations management is important for business students from a functional perspective and from an organizational systems approach. Students undertaking a business degree often have preconceived ideas relating to some business functions such as marketing, accountancy and personnel management, but are largely unaware or often uninterested in the notion of operations. Historically it is related to production management, operations research and engineering.

Rationale for the development

The development intended to provide both a constructive learning environment and a more meaningful experience for the students.

The syllabus for the unit built upon an introductory unit and introduced more quantitative aspects of the operations decision-making process, coupled with extending the organizational implications of these decisions. The content of the syllabus was to remain the same, but the process of delivering it, which was based on the traditional model of lecture and seminar, was to alter. The seminars were based on the analysis of case studies. Having random presentations, formal presentations, or in-class games or demonstrations provided variety. It was felt that the teaching method did not equip students well for the realities of operations in practice or capture the nature of the organizational analysis inherent within the unit. Pressures on resources were also limiting the amount of time staff were spending with students. The challenge to the tutor is to shape the resource model to enable students to receive a quality education and at the same time be flexible enough to cope with a variety of situations. Importantly, how best can we make use of the majority of time allocated for a unit that is spent normally outside the classroom?

Development process

In the early stages of the development, research involving books, journals, and computer information sources was used to put the development into context and examine similar developments in other fields. This research provided a template for the development. Information, gained from student and tutor surveys, is used to continually improve the unit.

The aims were to:

- cover part of the operations management subject area in a practical and applied manner;
- develop independent and autonomous learning;
- improve student performance;
- improve student perceptions of quality;
- aid in flexible learning initiatives;
- develop an alternative learning approach for students;
- facilitate uniformity of delivery;
- facilitate unambiguous assessment.

Four principles seemed appropriate to the learning objectives:

- experiential learning;
- continual formative assessment;
- instrumental teamwork;
- mentoring.

To achieve the aims a unit was developed that:

- was continually assessed;
- was peer assessed;
- provided formative assessment feedback through bespoke lectures;
- involved teamwork and mentoring;
- included very clear and extensive unit structure and learning materials;
- involved skills as well as information acquisition.

SIMULATING OPERATIONS MANAGEMENT

This section describes the development, implementation and operation of the new approach. Students, in groups of four, have to consider a number of issues within a scenario of actually setting up and running a business. An integrated case study, the OPSMAN Business Game (written for the programme) provides the case information as well as information technology (IT) tools to help in analysis.

Assessment

Assessment is an important area to generate motivation for the unit. Assessment of the module is formal and weekly. Each week the students are required to submit a report that describes their firm's response to a particular issue. Each report is approximately 800 words in length, with the accompanying results of any analysis undertaken. An individual final report of 500 words provides a personal reflection on the performance of the firm and how this performance might have been improved, as well as a critique of the unit itself. During the course of the unit each student provides approximately 3000 words of comment and participates in the analysis of 10 operations management problems. A model, created from the student responses, reflects the possible effects of the decision and creates a business profile that indicates profits. The model also caters for assessment and it keeps a running total of individual and group marks. Results are fed back to the students in the form of league tables. They can see their current mark and how their team was performing in relation to other groups.

The teaching and assessment process is shown in Figure 6.1.

Unit structure

Scheduled tutor contact is 15 hours per semester, irrespective of student numbers. The 15 hours are used to deliver five keynote lectures that highlight the key points related to the course, and 10 review and feedback sessions, which review the progress of the case study. Additionally three minutes per student, per week, is set aside for mentoring and assessment (ie, about 15 minutes per group per week). The support is controlled via an appointments system.

The materials developed for the unit

The written material needed to be of sufficient quality to enable both tutors and students to assimilate easily the teaching methods and requirements of the unit. This material is based on a house style (the International Modular Master's in Management Programme, IM3P). This style clearly indicates on a week-by-week basis the learning outcomes and requirements of each session. The materials supplied include a suite of computer resources, based on the Excel spreadsheet, for both learning and assessment.

The unit documentation is an essential part of the unit and includes two volumes: the *Tutor Guide and the Student Guide*. The *Tutor Guide* consists of:

- The Teaching and Learning Schedule: gives a detailed account of each week's activities and the learning outcomes expected. It indicates both student and tutor activity for lecture and feedback sessions. It indicates the resource list for individual sessions.

- The *Tutor Guide:* gives both lecture and feedback session guidance and includes session notes and overhead projector (OHP) masters. It gives a detailed description of the unit's assessment process.

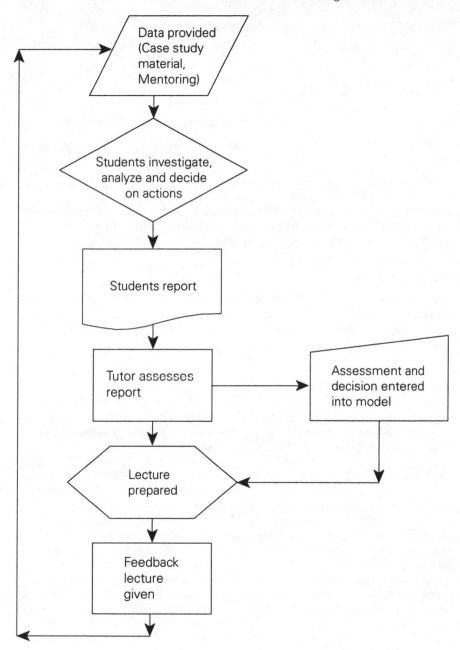

Figure 6.1 *The Teaching and Assessment Process*

- OPSMAN: game information sheets and software.

- OPSMAN: game instructor's notes – gives a detailed account of each week's topics and likely responses from the students.

The Student Guide consists of:

- The Teaching and Learning Schedule and assessment instructions;

- OPSMAN game: the information sheets and software.

Costs of development

The cost of the initial development was 120 hours of staff time (although in real terms at least twice as much time was devoted to the development). An improvement process has been continuing ever since.

The unit in action

The unit is used to teach on full and part-time undergraduate courses, as well as Master's and short programmes. All students are required to submit a questionnaire and an individual critical appraisal of the unit. Three members of staff have been involved with the delivery.

A TUTOR PERSPECTIVE

The new style of delivery was both a challenging and risky undertaking for the members of staff delivering the unit. The tutors in this case needed to deliver a lecture every other week and an assessment response session every week. Sixty-six students participated in the initial delivery of the unit. The tutors needed to assess 16 reports and create a lecture from these. Two hours a week were set aside for individual and group counselling and one hour allowed for assessment (three by 66 minutes). It quickly became evident that assessment would take longer than one hour a week. From an initial two hours the assessment grew to around three to four hours per week. Although arduous, it was enjoyable, especially when students had obviously put a lot of work into preparing a response.

Each week a new section of the case study is placed on the university's bulletin board system, together with any relevant software. The students download this and respond to the issues. This caused some problems, especially in the first week, with the volume of material printed stretching facilities. To counteract this, the documentation was compiled into a single volume and is now distributed at the beginning of the semester.

The initial response from the students during the first two weeks is normally one of high interest. Most students remained committed to the unit for the duration of the semester. Motivation is high, students in their groups of four discuss the unit in the canteen, or in the Union bar.

The tutor mentoring process started disappointingly. Few students used the opportunity to see the tutors, on a formal basis, for advice or guidance. The issue was raised after two weeks. Apparently, students were scared to use this facility for fear of getting a lower mark. Misunderstanding the unit material, which implied a 'cost' in using the tutor as a consultant, may have caused this. Only after it was explained that the mentoring process was not punitive did some students begin to ask for advice. The numbers, however, were still relatively small, and mainly consisted of students who were getting poorer marks. However, students did bypass the formal system and informal assistance was given regularly outside the office.

A cause of concern, for a small number of students, relates to the lack of attendance at both lectures and feedback sessions and poor team performance. Some students prefer to work as individuals, or are assessment focused. They will collect formal assignments at the start of the semester and comply with the minimum attendance requirements, providing little input into formal seminars, or teamwork. These students are penalized by this form of delivery, as it requires a continual involvement. However, operations management in practice relies heavily on teamwork, hence, it can be argued, is a valid learning outcome for the unit.

For intensive periods of study, the unit provides a vehicle to discuss subjects within the curriculum. What it can not do is duplicate the process the full-time students experienced, which was vastly different. For example, the intensively delivered programme does not cause the same level of involvement that is experienced by some of the full-timers.

Students at first find it difficult to write concisely. They also tend to keep to a narrow viewpoint. Students who worked as a team invariably produced the best results. The standard of reporting gradually improves over the course of the unit.

An unwritten objective of utilizing the tutor's time effectively was not realized initially. The time spent in preparation and assessment was greater than one would have experienced running the unit in a traditional manner. This is not surprising if one believes in the cliché 'no pain – no gain'. A process of learning for the tutors had to be undertaken. After the initial trial, changes in the way the unit is delivered have enabled more efficiency in this respect, without losing the integrative nature of the unit.

The demand on resources, in terms of room numbers, was reduced; fewer but larger rooms were required. The need for reprographic facilities increased. Previously students were only provided with a 10-page guide to the unit; the need now arose to provide 100-page document for each student. The cost of the associated documentation is about £2.00 per student.

Overall, in terms of the objectives for the unit, staff felt that most of them had been achieved and the unit provided an enhanced learning experience for the students at both undergraduate and postgraduate levels. Qualitatively this was apparent by the increased level of communication between staff and students and the increased level of discussion both in and out of the classroom. The remarks of the questionnaire back this up.

STUDENT PERFORMANCE

As the unit has developed, average performance has consistently been higher using the new method of teaching and with a greater range. A comparison of marks between years shows a reduction in the number of fails and an increase in the number of students getting marks above 70. This reflects three issues: the additional effort most students put into the unit; continual assessment that enabled students to recover if they received poor marks; and marking being generous at the start to encourage students to work at the new style of delivery. The range of marks perhaps indicates that the method distinguishes differences in individual performance more accurately.

STUDENT COMMENTS

Student comments were collected using a Likert-type questionnaire. The questionnaire requires students to rate aspects of the unit, as well as provide qualitative comments. In summary, the key issues addressed in this evaluation were as follows:

- peer assessment: was this liked?
- clash: how did the unit operate with other units?
- IT: did students find the models difficult to understand and use?
- content: was the material appropriate for the students' studies?
- suitability: would the approach useful for other units?
- workload: how easy or difficult was it to keep up with the work?
- work relevance: would the unit contribute to future career aspirations?
- interesting: was it?
- weekly assessment: was this useful?
- written materials: how useful were these?
- tutor contact: was there too much or too little, or just enough?
- compatibility: how well was the unit integrated with other units in the programme?
- skills: how well did the unit develop skills?

Some anomalies exist in the outcomes of the evaluation; for example, the students scored skills very highly, yet the IT element received a negative response.

Students found the unit interesting and enjoyable, despite the feeling that the workload was judged too high. One factor that retained their interest was the developmental nature of the case study. Being just a single case split into 10 sections, the students could relate to the unifying thread through the unit.

A few students did not like the unit; this may reflect the differing styles of learning that students enjoy or expect. The fact that most students enjoyed the unit would indicate that business students tend to be 'activist' in their learning styles. The highest score was in the improvement of skills, particularly teamwork.

Comments on the unit ranged from, 'I hate you for spoiling three months of my life' to 'thank you for the best course I have taken'. The former was, fortunately, in the minority.

FUTURE DEVELOPMENTS

The unit has evolved, based on the student responses and tutor experience. All the documentation is contained in a single volume that alleviates pressures on the computer centre. The assessment regime has been made more flexible, by reducing the number of formal assessments to five related to group work and a single piece of individual work. The spreadsheets have been made more user friendly.

The next stage of the development is to make the unit available to off-site tutors, or to partner institutions. These institutions range from other campuses within ULH to franchised colleges, and universities in eastern and western Europe. For many of the tutors concerned, it will be a radical change in teaching methods, which may be viewed with some trepidation. As House (1974: 34) explains:

> The personal costs of trying innovations are often high . . . and seldom is there any indication the innovations are worth the investment. They require one to believe that they will ultimately bear fruit and be worth the personal investment, often without the hope of a personal return. Costs are also high. The amount of energy and time required to learn the new skills and roles associated with the new innovation is a useful index to the magnitude of resistance.

Higher education is undergoing profound changes in the way that it operates. Staff are often bemused by the rationale for the changes, and fear hidden agendas. Academic staff generally have a degree of freedom in the way in which they deliver a syllabus. They can tailor the syllabus to suit their own style. Although staff welcome guidance on programme delivery, many would object to and ignore detailed instructions about content, process and procedure for individual sessions.

For this unit there is a risk of false clarity, ie the tutors being confused as to the rationale methodology and objectives of the unit. As Fullen (1991) suggests, false clarity occurs when a full realization of effects of change is not understood. In the case of this unit, the demands of assessment and feedback preparation can be arduous unless clearly explained and undertaken methodically.

CONCLUSIONS

This was an ambitious project, which aimed to provide an academically credible delivery of an established subject area, as well as provide associated skills. It also aimed to establish a critical and analytical approach to management decision making. To do this the unit was designed around established learning and psychological processes. Commitment to the learning process was established through the assessment regime. Motivation was developed through the integrated approach, and teamwork. Students were rewarded for process rather than correctness. For the majority of students this provided an enjoyable, interesting and worthwhile learning experience, which has provided them with learning and work-based skills. Of the many issues covered by this paper the most notable are:

- developing new teaching material needs careful planning with respect to audience, delivery, and assessment;

- developing new material will take longer than you expect;

- adopt a prototype approach to development. Development should not stop after the initial thrust, because all programmes need continual improvement;

- you cannot please all of the people all of the time, compromises need to be made;

- a single theme, clear aims, and continual assessment is motivational;

- mentoring is a useful aid in the learning process, but if not sought by students, it needs to be directed towards those who need it.

REFERENCES

Fullen, M (1991) *The New Meaning of Educational Change*, Cassell Educational Limited, London
House E (1974) quoted in Fullen M (1991), *The Meaning of Educational Change*, Cassell Educational Limited, London

7

Inspiring Students in a Health Studies Programme

Andréa Riesch Toepell

SUMMARY

Most students enrolled in the Introduction to Health Studies course at Brock University are not interested in the course materials. For the past three years, the professor (author) teaching this course has modified the presentation of material and structure of the assignments in an effort to better engage the uninspired student.

Strategies adopted include:

- applying the materials to the students' own experience;
- devising assignments to develop transferable skills;
- presenting material using a variety of methods.

Success in applying such new strategies has been noted in improved course evaluations and overall satisfaction among students enrolled in the course.

INTRODUCTION

The following paragraphs describe the university, department and the course under examination in more detail. An overview as to why uninspired students are found enrolled in the Introduction to Health Studies course is provided.

The institution

Brock University is located in southern Ontario. It lies in the Niagara Peninsula, an area known for its orchards and vineyards. The university is medium sized with 13,000 full- and part-time students. It is primarily an undergraduate university, with a few graduate programmes offered in certain departments.

There are 16 other universities across the province, and only three offer a programme of study in the field of health sciences that is comparable to the health studies programme at Brock University.

The Department of Health Studies

The programmes in health studies are offered in response to a growing interest in health-related issues. The curriculum integrates knowledge from several traditional disciplines. Courses focus on the investigation of health maintenance and the development of positive health from both behavioural and biological perspectives.

Both a BA in Health Studies and a BSc in Health Sciences are offered. The BA Health Studies pass programme (three years) focuses on community health and wellness with an emphasis on health promotion, programme development and evaluation, and health assessment. The BA Health Studies honours programme (four years) provides the opportunity for a more intensive examination of issues in health and wellness than is offered in the BA pass programme.

The BSc Health Science programme prepares students for careers in health professions with a bio-science focus. This degree allows students to meet the requirements for the postgraduate degree programme of their choice.

In both degrees a core of health studies courses are supplemented by a broad choice of electives from other university departments. Students who wish to study in particular areas of interest select appropriate elective courses to prepare them to meet their academic and career goals.

The courses offered in health studies/science

The health studies programme offers a wide range of courses, some of which are core (mandatory for a completed degree) and others elective to complement the number of required credits for either a three- or four-year degree. The following is an example of the areas of study offered:

- research methods and statistical evaluation;
- health and wellness in Canada;
- gerontology;
- healthy communities;
- human sexuality;
- health promotion;
- gender and health;
- programme planning and development;
- nutrition;
- anatomy;

- community health assessment;

- processes of health and wellness.

Regardless of which degree students are enrolled in (BA versus BSc) or the type of degree they intend to complete (pass versus honours), all students must complete the introductory course to the programme. This course is entitled Introduction to Health Studies and students must achieve a minimum of 60 per cent as their final grade before being eligible to declare themselves a health studies major.

The introductory course

The introductory course is a first-year level course and is typically taken during a student's first year of study. The course establishes a foundation upon which the curriculum for subsequent courses in the programme is built. For example, in this first-year course discussions concerning ageing, sexuality, and healthy communities are introduced, and these topics can be later pursued in courses offered in second and third year.

The introductory course provides the student with an overview of the historical development and current situation of federal, provincial and local health care systems in Canada; health status of Canadians; controversies and issues in the area of health; and an introduction to Canadian legislation concerning health and wellness. Students also develop critical analysis skills which they must demonstrate in both written and verbal forms. Students are also encouraged to explore personal opinions and beliefs through critical reflection when examining controversial issues.

The course is designed in such a way that at its conclusion, students are able to demonstrate the following:

- an appreciation for the complexities involved in the concept of health and current Canadian health issues;

- an awareness of current health trends and issues facing Canadians;

- an appreciation of the diversity of opinion surrounding issues in health;

- effective verbal communication skills;

- listening skills during dialogue, discussion and debate;

- critical analysis skills;

- an ability to participate in an informed manner in class discussions;

- searching for and retrieving research articles from the library.

These objectives are met by attending lectures and seminars, completing assignments, and taking written examinations.

The structure of the course includes a weekly two-hour lecture followed by a one-hour seminar (tutorial) and runs the full academic year (ie 24 weeks).

Information is presented to the students in lecture format. During these presentations, students are encouraged to ask questions and stimulate discussion. Weekly readings are assigned and are 'required readings'. Students are expected to come prepared to all classes (lectures and seminars), having read the readings assigned for the week, and to attend all seminars. The purpose of the lectures is not to reiterate the readings, but to further develop and augment the content of the readings. More intimate and explorative group discussions and activities are conducted in the seminars.

The nature and numbers of students

Since the course is offered at the first-year level, registration is open to all students across the campus. That is, students in any undergraduate year level (from first to fourth year) and from any discipline may take the Introduction to Health Studies course. As a result, a large mix of students take the course. For the past three years, enrolment has reached 400. The university's largest lecture hall can only seat 400 students, otherwise even more students would be enrolled. Despite its popularity, the majority of students on the course are uninspired by its content, the two reasons for which are explained below.

First, at Brock University all first-year students are required to take one introductory course from each of the fields of humanities, social sciences, natural sciences, English and arts. Courses taken in order to fulfil this requirement are known as 'core and context' courses, of which five must be taken at the first-year level. The Introduction to Health Studies course is one of the few courses that is eligible to fulfil the social science core and context requirement – regardless of what a student's major might be. Therefore, most students in this course are taking it because it fulfils a university requirement for their completed degree.

Second, many upper year students mistakenly assume that a first-year course, and one that is 'introductory', is an easier and less demanding course than others offered at second year and up. Therefore, there is an appeal to enrol in first year courses when trying to balance a workload that includes second-, third- and/or fourth-year level courses. However, it is a known fact that first-year level courses are typically much more demanding and require even more preparation for lecture and examinations than other level year courses. In the case of the Introduction to Health Studies course, a large amount of material is covered in both the readings and lectures.

The type of students enrolled in the Introduction to Health Studies course can be divided into two groups: those who wish or are considering to major in health studies, and those not interested in majoring in the programme but who are taking the course as core and context or as an elective.

Half of the students in the course are true first-year students (ie, in their first year of study at the university), the remaining half are second-, third- and fourth-year students. Of the first-year students taking the course, approximately half are considering becoming a major in health studies, while the other half are unsure of their choice of major or are certain they will not major in this particular programme. Therefore, the teacher expects that only 100 of the 400 students on the course are interested in the subject (possible majors) and are perhaps the most inspired students. In other words, up to 300 students in the course may be completely uninterested in the course material, but are nevertheless on the course because it fulfils a core and context degree requirement, appears to be a light-loaded course, or best fits their class schedule.

The teacher faces a challenge when trying to keep the course material inspiring and exciting when potentially three-quarters of the student body in class are remotely interested in the subject area. Clearly, more effort must go into making the course material absorbing for a larger group of students who likely will not continue their studies in the health studies programme than for students who are genuinely inspired by the course content.

IMPLICATIONS OF UNINSPIRED STUDENTS IN CLASS

As experienced in the Introduction to Health Studies course, students who are not interested in course materials tend not to pay attention in lectures, do not participate in seminars, do poorly on assignments and examinations, and negatively evaluate the course at the end of term.

Students who feel obliged to attend lectures and are uninterested in the materials presented can often create a disturbance for other students and the teacher. More chatting takes place between students during lectures when the material is not captivating enough for the uninspired student. Disruptive behaviours make it much more difficult for other students to follow the lecture and pay attention to the materials presented. Further, such disruptions are distracting to the teacher, especially when the instructor must interrupt the lecture in order to address disorderly behaviour.

Uninspired students tend to also be uncooperative or unmotivated to participate in discussion during seminar times. It is not a fulfilling experience for other students who would appreciate full participation from all those attending the seminar. When a cluster of students is uninvolved in the group process, poorer learning takes places and negativity is felt by most.

Less attendance at lectures invariably results in poorer performance in examinations, particularly when the majority of lectures are missed. Uninspired students are not motivated to collect notes for missed lectures, and, hence, have fewer notes from which to study when preparing for examinations. Also, less effort is put towards completing assignments, thereby resulting in poorer scores and overall lower final grades at the completion of the course. If most of the class is uninterested in the course material and most students do poorly in examinations and assignments, then the final grade distribution for the course is negatively skewed.

Generally when students perform poorly in a course, the overall consensus (from the students' perspective) is that course or instructor – or both – was overly difficult. It is then less likely that such students will give a positive course evaluation. As described previously, given that most students in this course are not keenly interested in the material, the overall course evaluation scores are low despite the averaging of scores. Such trends reflect negatively on the course professor, despite all efforts made to motivate students, which ultimately taints the professor's record of teaching evaluations.

Finally, the less interested the students are in the course, the less motivated and enthusiastic is the teacher. Uninspired students can easily make instructors feel equally uninspired to teach, especially when up to three-quarters of the students are on the course simply to fulfil a degree requirement.

FINDING WAYS TO INSPIRE STUDENTS

Some strategies used to inspire students in the Introduction to Health Studies course include:

- creatively applying the material to the students' own personal experience;

- devising assignments that help to develop transferable skills to other courses;

- presenting material in a variety of methods to best meet students' individual learning styles;

- finding techniques to present material in exciting and inspiring ways.

Discovering learning styles and how no one teaching style suits all students can be positive for all involved (Blume, 1992), as students have a better chance of success in courses that meet several learning styles (Toepell, 1998). Although much is written that describes student learning styles and instructor's teaching styles, Table 7.1 outlines Kolb's (1984) learning cycle when understanding students' learning process, and his four phases of learning.

Svinicki and Dixon (1987) suggest possible activities best suited for the above phases of learning, as outlined in Table 7.2.

In the case of the Introduction to Health Studies course, each learning phase and preference type is given attention through various activities presented in the course. For example, films and videos are shown during some lectures, discussion and questioning are encouraged during lecture and seminar time (especially when trying to foster critical thinking skills), written assignments are part of the course requirements, and students work together on case studies and facilitation projects during seminar time.

When students are not interested in the content of a lecture or the course overall, it is likely because they feel the material is not relevant to their life or experiences. A seminar leader can change such an attitude by demonstrating the relevance of the material by applying it to the personal experiences of students. Dry and uninspiring materials must be presented to students in ways that illustrate meaning and importance, and this is best done by personalizing material to their past or future experiences. For example, this process of application is used in the course to demonstrate how legislation concerning tobacco, alcohol or illicit drug use will later impact on a student's freedoms and choices. Or, predicting how the funding and programming structures affecting health care for the elderly today will change over time (likely for the

Table 7.1 *Kolb's learning cycle*

Phase of learning	Processes at this phase
Concrete experience (feeling)	– learning from specific experiences – learning from feeling – relating to people – sensitivity to feelings and people
Reflective observation (watching)	– careful observation before making a judgement – viewing things from different perspectives – looking for the meaning of things – learning by watching and listening
Abstract conceptualization (thinking)	– learning by thinking – logical analysis of ideas – systematic planning – acting on an intellectual understanding of a situation
Active experimentation (doing)	– learning by doing – ability to get things done – risk taking – influencing people and events through action

Table 7.2 *Activities best suited for Kolb's phases of learning*

Phase of learning	Class activities at this phase
Concrete experience (feeling)	– films – games – fieldwork – laboratory work – observation
Reflective observation (watching)	– journals – discussion – questioning
Abstract conceptualization (thinking)	– building models – writing papers – creating analogies
Active experimentation (doing)	– case studies – projects – simulations

worse) will eventually impact on the quality of care the students will receive when they become senior citizens. At times this approach requires one to over-generalize or assume the experiences of student life.

When the content of a course cannot be modified in order to make the materials more captivating to students, the application of the theory taught or logic discussed should be made outside the context of the course. For example, in the introductory course for health studies, issues are examined with the intent to develop good critical thinking skills. Such skills are applicable outside of class, as they are skills used in everyday life – although to most students thinking critically is a new approach.

Also, developing effective debating skills requires good listening and communication skills, both of which are best developed when arguing controversial issues. Opportunities must be created that enable students to build on such skills. In the case of the health studies course, it is during seminar time when students debate contentious issues such as abortion, legalization of illicit drug use, AIDS, euthanasia, etc – and nurture good communication skills and critical thinking development.

Assignments must also be created that require students to develop skills that are transferable to assignments in other courses on campus. In the Introduction to Health Studies course students are required to write several discussion papers throughout the year. These papers are a critical reflection of the readings assigned for a particular week. The purpose of the papers is to provide the students with opportunities to develop effective writing skills and critical analysis skills – both of which are necessary for papers written for other university courses. Other assignments require students to critique peer-reviewed and popular media health articles. The purpose of these critiques is to apply the skills developed during the writing of discussion papers when comparatively critiquing published articles in the health field. Again, the skills of such exercises are likely to be applicable to other course requirements outside of health studies.

In this course, seminar participation is graded based on the involvement and quality of input students bring to seminars. They are responsible for bringing new and/or challenging ideas to seminars and for actively participating in the discussion and activities. Each week a new student is responsible for facilitating the discussion and learning process. Again, opportunities for developing discussion and leadership skills must be made available to students; however, it is helpful to make explicitly clear to them that these skills are transferable outside of the course and that such skills will also serve students well beyond their academic lives.

When teaching uninspired students, it is important to bear in mind that each student has his or her own learning style and that disinterest in course material may be a reflection of an ineffective teaching style. It is best to present material in as many varying ways and styles as possible. In the case of the Introduction to Health Studies course, every week the lecture material is presented in multiple formats in order to best captivate the attention of 400 students. These formats include: lecturing; generating discussion with students by asking them questions during lectures and seminars; multimedia presenta-

tions including overheads both prepared in advance and ones that are drawn/
constructed during the lecture; computer-generated presentations; films, music
videos, lyrics from music, and cartoons; and occasional guest speakers. Such a
variety of information presentation media and speakers will help to draw even
the most uninspired student into the course material.

The instructor should also consider creative ways to demonstrate or reinforce
course content. For example, the six dimensions of health (mental, physical,
social, emotional, environmental, spiritual) are the cornerstone to the courses,
and the rock video entitled 'Another day in paradise' by Phil Collins is used to
provide a visual illustration of how these dimensions of health are compromised
among the many homeless, disabled, poor, and ethnically varied populations
in the United States. The lyrics from the song 'We didn't start the fire' written
by Billy Joel help to highlight how history has positively and negatively influenced determinants of our health nationally and internationally (for example,
the discovery of Terylene (Dacron), contraception, thalidomide, war, nuclear
warfare, HIV, racial discrimination, suicide, etc). Neither the video nor the
music were created with the Introduction to Health Studies course in mind,
but were applied later. This strategy not only captured the students' interest,
but it was a vehicle by which they could more easily comprehend, apply and
retain course content.

Finally, instructors must try at all costs to make their course content as
exciting or interesting as possible. Applying the discussion of materials to the
experiences of students is a good method to capture attention, although it is
the instructor's enthusiasm for the material that maintains the students' interest.
At times remaining enthusiastic about lecture material when the behaviour of
the attending students indicate that they would rather be elsewhere can be a
challenge for even the most seasoned teacher. Appropriate use of humour and
expressing genuine concern about students' performance in the course
are additional strategies that make uninspired students keep an open mind
concerning their attitudes or prejudices toward the course.

KEY LESSONS

It must be understood that not everyone enrolled in a particular course is
necessarily interested in the material and content. Students enrol in courses
for various reasons, not all of which are clear to the instructor.

When teachers become aware that students are uninspired by course content,
they must find creative ways of demonstrating how the material relates to the
realities of students' experiences. The instructor should also make explicitly
clear how study strategies and skills developed when completing assignments
will assist them in other courses and later life.

It is also beneficial for instructors to make the connections between theories,
concepts, materials, etc very clear, as this makes it easier for those whose interest
is waning to keep on track. Further, making such connections helps unmotivated
students to see the relevance of course content, thereby encouraging them to
take more interest in their studies.

Above all, teachers should try never to lose enthusiasm for teaching the content of a course. Enthusiasm and genuine excitement can help turn around the uninspired, and, besides, enthusiasm is catching!

CONCLUSIONS

Almost all introductory first-year courses are the largest-sized classes for departments. Very large classes pose particular difficulties over very small classes. It is much more challenging to capture and maintain everyone's interest in a large and fully occupied lecture hall than it is in a small and intimate class of a few students. It must be understood by instructors of such courses that it is impossible to satisfy all the learning preferences and interests of each student; however, instructors are not immobilized to make the experience as pleasant and valuable as possible for everyone involved.

REFERENCES

Blume, S (1992) Learning styles, in *Your College Experience: Strategies for success*, eds JN Gardner and AJ Jewler, Wadsworth Publishers, CA

Kolb, DA (1984) *Experiential Learning: Experiences as a source of learning and development*, Prentice-Hall, NJ

Svinicki, MD and Dixon, NM (1987) Kolb model modified for classroom activities, *College Teaching*, **35**, pp 141–46

Toepell, AR (1998) Paralleling the experiences of first year professors and freshmen, *Academic Exchange Quarterly*, **2**, pp 32–45

8

Introducing Computing and Information Systems

Jonathan Lean, Terry Mangles and Jonathan Moizer

SUMMARY

This chapter examines the use of a computer-based business simulation or 'game' in the teaching of computing and information systems to business students. The main interests of such students are generally in such areas as marketing, personnel management and finance.

The simulation described was developed to provide an engaging and integrating learning experience for students while at the same time meeting the primary module objective: facilitating the attainment of computing and information management skills and knowledge.

An evaluation of the simulation, based upon focus group interviews with students, has been conducted to explore its perceived value as a learning tool. Findings indicate that the module is broadly successful in achieving its aims, although some areas for future development are revealed. Equally importantly, the game engages the attention of the students, whatever their main subject interest.

INTRODUCTION

First-year students at the University of Plymouth Business School study a range of core compulsory modules covering such areas as marketing, human resource management, economics, accounting and quantitative methods. Those students on the BA in Business Studies wishing to specialize in a particular aspect of business can go on to study for a BA in Marketing, Personnel Management or Business with Finance in subsequent years. These subjects represent the main areas of interest for the majority of students within the faculty. However, the business school has a strong belief that all of its graduates should be capable of working within a modern, computerized business environment. Therefore it also runs compulsory core modules in Computing Information Systems (CIS) for its major business programmes.

The key challenge facing staff teaching the first-year CIS modules is to provide a learning experience that all students will find engaging and useful for their future studies and careers, even though their main interests lie outside computing in such diverse areas as marketing, personnel, finance and even perfumery. The educational and work experiences of students participating in the course are wide ranging, and accommodating students with varying levels of knowledge and ability is an important consideration. However, the most fundamental issue is to provide a course which achieves its own objectives while also reflecting the wide range of preferred specialisms of participating students.

The institution

The University of Plymouth is one of the largest providers of higher education in the United Kingdom, with around 21,000 students (18,500 at undergraduate level). It has four large campuses located at Exeter, Exmouth, Plymouth and Newton Abbot. Access to higher education in the region is further enhanced by links with 20 partner colleges in Cornwall, Devon and Somerset, offering diploma and degree courses in a wide range of subjects. The university is a major contributor to the economic wealth of the region and is closely involved in the development of new business opportunities. It also strives to develop transferable business skills among students across its various programmes.

The business school

The school offers a comprehensive portfolio of award programmes including a range of specialist undergraduate degrees, professional qualifications, taught MBA and Master's programmes and research degrees. All programmes are delivered within a modular and semester format, and are designed to provide students with a flexible and challenging learning experience. The academic staff expertise is focused upon accounting, business operations and strategy, economics, human resource management, law, marketing and modern languages.

The 'BABS' and 'BABA' programmes

The two major undergraduate programmes that include CIS modules are the BA in Business Studies (BABS) and the BA in Business Administration (BABA). The business simulation described in this study has been used on both programmes. The BABS degree is well established at the business school and is run as a four-year sandwich course. It is a modular scheme that allows students to specialize in later years, typically in either marketing, personnel management or finance. The three-year BABA programme was introduced in 1997/98 and aims to develop graduate attributes that are transferable to the wider world of business (see, for example, Otter, 1997) through a strong commitment to student-centred independent learning (SCIL). The new BABA follows a common programme of study that emphasizes the practical application of skills (allied to traditional academic disciplines) with students developing a portfolio of consultancy-style work in their final year.

The students

First-year BABA students are typically recent Sixth Form leavers with 12 or more A level points (grade A=10 points, B=8 points, C=6 points, D=4 points and E=2 points). This compares to a requirement of 18 or more points for BABS. Given the relatively low entry requirements for BABA and the fact that it is a three-year course, it is expected that there will be an increase in the number of mature student applicants in future years. During 1997/98 there were 110 BABA students, while BABS typically enrols around 300, 10 per cent of whom are over 21.

THE CONTEXT

Research conducted with employers by the University of Plymouth (*Ethos Newsletter*, 1995) has shown that employers wish to see a range of different skills in the graduates they employ. In addition to the possession of embedded basic core disciplines (providing an understanding of technical detail) and the ability to flexibly transfer skills rooted in specific knowledge, a number of generic transferable skills were also identified. These included interpersonal, presentational, communication, leadership and teamwork skills. Rated most important however were information technology (IT) skills. This finding is reflected in the Dearing Report (NCIHE, 1997), which states:

> . . . changes [in information technology] have important implications for higher education. They affect the types of skills which students will have when they enter higher education, their expectations of the facilities and learning modes open to them and the types of skills and intellectual attributes which those leaving higher education will need to have if they are to operate successfully in the modern world. For example, the development of high-level skills in handling the large volumes of complex information which can be made available by communications technology will be one of the tasks of undergraduate programmes.

While the challenge to develop transferable skills is pertinent to all disciplines, it is particularly so in business-related programmes which are, by their nature, expected to deliver rounded and vocationally well-equipped graduates. Furthermore, research indicates that even among the smallest of firms, the use of IT is widespread and increasing (McClure and Blackburn, 1997). It is therefore regarded as critical that all business school graduates are proficient in the use of common business applications and understand their role in aiding business decision making.

THE PROBLEM

A number of challenges exist in teaching computing modules to business students. First, as already suggested, the ultimate aim of many business school students is to specialize in such areas as marketing and personnel. Therefore computing falls outside their main area of interest. Second, and of increasing significance, is that growing numbers of students entering the first year already have some experience in using computer applications. Many therefore perceive that they 'already know computing', despite the fact that their experience is often limited to a little word processing, some basic spreadsheet work and the use of the Internet. In reality, only a small number have very high level skills. A failure among students to recognize their own limitations in the use of computer applications within business scenarios is for some reflected in disappointing assessment grades. A further group of students are those who still have practically no experience in using computer applications, although this is a small and shrinking minority. Thus the range of abilities within a typical cohort is wide.

The main challenges arising from the nature of students being taught are to provide a module that:

- emphasizes the real world integration of computer systems into the various functions of business (finance, marketing, operations, personnel), thus inspiring the interest of all students, whatever their preferred functional area;

- accommodates students with varying levels of knowledge and ability;

- provides a thorough and in-depth understanding of the use of specific computer applications and the development of business-focused systems;

- helps students appreciate the holistic nature of the business, and the idea that cooperation between interdependent system actors can give rise to synergy benefits.

THE SOLUTION: A COMPUTER-BASED BUSINESS SIMULATION

The CIS module being evaluated in this study utilizes an interactive computer-based business game/simulation designed within the faculty called 'Aromatherapy Candles'. It aims to help students to develop IT skills and their basic understanding of the role of CIS in businesses. Through this group-centred game, IT skills are augmented in the context of a variety of management roles and situations that are closely linked to the students' main areas of interest. In each group, students take on the role of sales manager, production manager, accountant or managing director of a firm producing aromatherapy candles. Following a single introductory lecture and with the help of specially written guided learning materials (Mangles, 1998), each has to develop a computer-based information system to support their decision making and assist them in the week-to-week running of their company. An e-mail system is used as the primary means of communication between 'managers'.

The simulation is run in a large computer laboratory generally with 36 students and one lecturer. As the simulation is completely automated, the role of the lecturer is that of facilitator and troubleshooter when, for example, technical problems arise. In each two-hour session, between one and four simulated playing weeks are run. The simulation is generally run across six teaching sessions. The real-time duration of each playing week can be decreased (using a computer password) as students gain in confidence and experience. During each playing week, orders are generated by the aromatherapy candles computer system (referred to the Umpire System as it also records all the decisions made by each company) and placed with the student companies. The sales manager then makes a quote for each order via the Umpire System. This then informs the sales manager which quotes have been accepted. Where quotes are accepted, the company has to produce the necessary candles and deliver them on time, also producing a full set of accounts (using a computer application) for each week.

A number of parameter constraints exist in the simulation that the company must work within. For example, production constraints relating to the amount of melting and setting possible within the candle factory exist. Production managers are required to develop a computer-based stock control system to enable them to plan production, manage inventory and provide information inputs to other managers. Meanwhile, the sales manager has to develop a sales monitoring system, the accountant an average cost system, and the general manager an overall design for the company's information system. All must be developed using appropriate software.

Students are also expected to use the computer systems to analyse data generated in the areas of production, sales and finance using appropriate statistical or graphical techniques. A variety of problems and hazards are also presented to the groups throughout the game. Again, these constraints and problems are related to the students' main areas of interest. For instance, a strike occurs during one week of the simulation and needs to be responded to (of interest to personnel students), while in another a market research report is presented to the firm for interpretation (of interest to marketing students).

At the end of the simulation, students produce a group report reflecting on their work, outlining the computer-based systems they have developed and showing their analysis of data. They are also required to give a presentation using a software application commonly used for computer-based business presentations.

The anticipated outcome of the module is that students develop both specific software skills (using e-mail, spreadsheet/data analysis, word processing and graphical/presentational applications) in an applied business context and that they develop a range of more generic skills. These include teamworking and the identification, analysis, interpretation and effective presentation of relevant data. Students should also develop an understanding of the integrative role of information systems within organizations, in particular gaining practical insights into how the different functions within a business (which may or may not be a particular student's main area of interest) relate to one another.

EVALUATION

The module described has been evaluated using funding from the University of Plymouth's Educational Development Service made available to investigate innovative approaches to teaching and learning within the university, particularly in the areas of technology and flexible learning. The main aim of the evaluation was to explore students' perceptions of the usefulness of the business simulation in terms of their learning experiences.

Methodology

Six 'focus group' interviews were conducted with students who had completed the business simulation. Focus groups consisted of four students who had worked together as a team during the module. Each focus group was conducted using a semi-structured format (Robson, 1993). Using this approach, an interview question guide is used, establishing the direction and scope of discourse while allowing a degree of flexibility to be maintained in the interactions between researcher and focus group interviewees. Questions asked related to their experiences and preconceptions of educational simulations, the success of the simulation in achieving the learning objectives of the module, the advantages and disadvantages of the learning approach and how the simulation could be improved (a copy of the guide is provided in Appendix 8.1, pages 71–72).

In order to elicit honest responses from all participants, it was felt necessary to ensure that there was a relaxed and open atmosphere during focus group sessions. To facilitate this, refreshments were provided in a non-hostile setting and focus groups were led by staff not directly involved in the teaching of the students in the group. Also, efforts were made to include all students in the discussion by asking each participant an 'ice-breaker' question at the start of the session. All focus group sessions were tape recorded and fully transcribed.

Results

An analysis of focus group transcripts shows that a small number of students had some limited prior experience of simulation-based learning in areas such as politics and accounting, though in all cases simulations were run over short time periods. There was general consensus among the students with regard to their preconceptions of simulations. They felt that simulations are fun and a welcome change to more traditional lecture-based teaching. After their introductory lecture, many students did however feel that they had been overloaded with information and were awaiting their first simulation session with some trepidation. Indeed, experience of running the sessions made it apparent that students' immediate concerns over operational aspects of the game did act to obscure its underlying objectives for a number of students during the initial weeks of the simulation. However, given that a key aim of the exercise was to provide students with practical experience in managing, analysing and acting upon large quantities of information, this was seen as an important aspect of the learning experience. Indeed, although all students were fully briefed on the objectives of the module during the introductory lecture, focus group responses show that for many students, the objectives of the simulation only really became clear during the latter part of the exercise as students began to reflect upon their experiences.

Similarly, for most of the simulation, the learning that occurred did so at a subconscious level. In other words, learning occurred as a result of their practical work as students considered how computer applications might be utilized to enhance the quality of their decision making and the performance of their business. The following quotes typify comments made by students:

'At the beginning it was all very confusing and we didn't have a clue what was going on. It was a gradual process. In the end it was very, very successful. It just took time.'

'It gets you involved instead of just turning up and sitting there passively . . . it really makes you get on with it and look at what you're doing and I think it makes you progress more than lectures do. I take more in when I do things in practice, in lectures I sort of sit there and go to sleep!'

'I liked the way I picked up so many things without realizing – because if you think "I've got to learn this" you just tend to block out things, but if you're doing it yourself you don't realize that you're learning. You learn more.'

These responses in part reflect Everett's (1989) model of learning. He suggests that the higher the level of participation in learning, the more participants remember. Students tend to remember more when learning and experience occur through actual performance, simulating actual performance, participation in a task, viewing a demonstration of a task and use of visual and audio material. The more active the student is, the more likely the retention of knowledge or skills.

It was also clear from the focus groups that most learning occurred either subconsciously (particularly in the case of specific software skills) or upon reflection. This reflective learning in some cases did not occur until students began to prepare their reports and presentations. However, given that this learning was firmly embedded in their own practical experience, students' understanding of issues and concepts relating to organizational information systems was in most cases clearer and deeper than might otherwise have been expected:

'I learnt more doing the presentation than sitting there each week. [I learnt when] preparing the slides and the overheads. When you're doing something you don't really think about it, you just do it automatically, but when you look back . . . you think why you did it.'

The provision of an effective mechanism for reflection is clearly critical to the success of this business simulation. Without this, the learning experience is incomplete. In the case of a minority of students, this mechanism was not effectively used and this was reflected in lower grades and a less positive attitude towards the game. Frequently, it was those groups whose businesses did less well financially that found it difficult to reflect positively upon their learning experiences. A critical lesson for staff is to underline the fact that the game is not a competition and that the financial performance of individual companies has no bearing on a group's ability to do well in the module.

A further set of distractions for some students were the technical hiccups that arose on occasions during the simulation, mostly relating to the operation of e-mail. Such technical failures, while teaching students valuable lessons about the vulnerabilities of computer systems, did have a de-motivating effect. The need for fallback activities when systems fail is an important short-term lesson, while over the longer term the need to enhance the robustness of systems under conditions of heavy usage is apparent.

CONCLUSION

Findings from focus group interviews with students show that the module is broadly successful in achieving its aims, although some areas for future development are highlighted. Evidence suggests that the way that students develop an understanding of concepts relating to business information systems through the course is different to conventional modes of learning. In particular, a range of technical and analytical skills are developed through hands-on, activity-focused practical experience. Less tangible knowledge-based competencies are meanwhile developed upon reflection, towards the end of the module. The experiential nature of the work undertaken leads to deeper learning. Equally as important, the game does engage the attention of the majority of students, whatever their main subject interest. This is because the course encourages them to conceptualize the business as a system, where each 'business function' (whether it be marketing, finance, production or personnel) is interrelated. Thus the individual student is able to identify more clearly the role of his or her particular area of interest within the business as a whole, generating enthusiasm and interest.

Key lessons that have emerged from the work presented in this chapter include:

- Simulations can provide an effective way of introducing experiential learning into the classroom. Learning does not occur in the same way as in the lecture theatre and is often subconscious or only recognized upon reflection.

- Due to its experiential nature, learning is often deeper than might be expected if conventional approaches were adopted. As it is different, it is also perceived to be more fun by students.

- For desired learning outcomes to be achieved, mechanisms for students to reflect upon their experiences must be put in place. It is also important to reinforce the overall purpose of the module to avoid students losing sight of their own objectives as they become involved in the operational aspects of the simulation.

- Simulations can provide a means of integrating subject matter into the mainstream of students' interests, providing an engaging and inspirational learning experience that adopts an holistic approach.

- Using technology as a means of facilitating learning can result in increased levels of vulnerability to disruption as a result of technical failures. Adequate measures should be taken to avoid such failures and particular attention should be paid to developing contingency plans in case failures occur.

REFERENCES

Ethos Newsletter (1995) Graduate skills survey, University of Plymouth, December issue

Everett, B (1989) Training techniques that work within an integrated safety program, *Professional Safety*, **34** (5), pp 34–37

Mangles, T (1998) *Aromatherapy Candles Business and Management Game*, University of Plymouth Business School

McClure, R and Blackburn, R (1997) The use of information and communications technologies in small business service firms, paper presented at the 20th Institute of Small Business Affairs, Small Firms Policy and Research Conference, Belfast, November

NCIHE (1997) (Dearing Report) *Higher Education in the Learning Society*, National Committee of Inquiry into Higher Education, HMSO, London

Otter, S (1997) *The Ability Based Curriculum*, Department for Education and Employment, London

Robson, C (1993) *Real World Research*, Blackwell Publishers, Oxford

APPENDIX 8.1
ATC GAMING SIMULATION
FOCUS GROUP QUESTION PLAN

Structure of the group

Groups containing four first-year business studies or business information systems students were selected randomly from a Computer Information Systems module at Plymouth Business School. They were invited to participate in a structured group discussion.

Ice-breaker

What did you do before you came to university and why did you decide to study business?

Familiarity with business games

What games or simulations, if any, have you played in your education?
Tell us about your experiences?

Preconceptions about business games

Think back to the start of the module, what were your view about learning from games as compared to conventional lectures?

Objective achievement

- After the initial talk what were your feelings about the game?

- What did you see as the main objective of the game (learning objectives of module)?

- At what stage of the game did the objectives become clear?

- How successful was the game in meeting those objectives?

- At what stage during the game were these objectives achieved (click point)?

Learning experience

- What did you learn about the role of information in a business?

- In what ways was the game good at making you think about how to use information in a business?

- What were the limitations of the game in exploring the role of information?

- Are the issues raised in the game relevant to the real world of business?

- Having played the game, in what ways are computer simulation games better for learning than structured lectures?

- In what ways was it worse?

- What do you think about using IT as a vehicle for learning?

- What do students need to do to learn from the game?

- In what others ways might learning be enhanced in the context of the game?

9

Introducing Communication Skills

Susan Nichols

SUMMARY

This chapter describes the use of group project work with first-year topics for engineering students. The particularly novel feature of the approach described is the fact that only staff from outside the engineering school teach the programme.

Students participate in a range of activities designed to develop the written and oral communication skills necessary to succeed in collaborative project work and subsequent employment.

The chapter describes the students' initial attitude to the topic and approach, outlines the communications component and offers some evidence of successful outcomes resulting in inspiration.

INTRODUCTION

'Engineers do not know how to communicate.' This provocative statement was made by a former director of medical engineering in an article aimed at prompting clinical engineers to change their attitude towards communicating with other professionals and the general public (Harrington, 1996). The drive to improve communication skills in industry does not apply only to engineering. Employer bodies in Australia and elsewhere frequently comment on the import-ance of writing, oral communication in industry and the comparative lack of these skills in university graduates (Spencer, 1998). However, engineering faculties may face a particular challenge if, as has been claimed, first-year engineering students are less skilled in literacy than arts or social science students (Robinson and Blair, 1995).

The call for improved communication skills for engineering students is part of a broader emphasis on collaborative problem solving, a curriculum approach which can more effectively simulate the 'real-life' world of a working engineer (Hadgraft, 1993; Hessami and Gani, 1993; Van Driel *et al*, 1997). Engineering courses are increasingly requiring students to work in teams to complete design, project or experimental tasks.

Introducing a communications component to the engineering curriculum also encourages the high-quality presentation of engineering information to audiences. Report writing and public speaking are seen as essential presentation skills for professional engineers.

The communications topic reported here was introduced as part of a curriculum reform process for first-year engineering at Flinders University and the University of South Australia in 1993 (Downing *et al*, 1993). The reforms had the general aim of increasing student motivation and, as a result, student retention. Improving student communication skills has been a crucial aspect of producing students who are both confident and attuned to the professional demands of engineering.

The curriculum context

Team Project and Communication Skills is a core topic in the first-year engineering course at Finders University. All work in the topic centres on the production of project reports by teams of eight students working collaboratively over one semester.

Each team of students works under the guidance of a team leader drawn from industry. Teams hold regular meetings to make decisions on strategies for researching and writing up their project topic. They are required both to produce a publication standard final report and to present their findings in a formal oral presentation.

Effective communication skills are crucial to achievement in this topic. In their team meetings, students need to be able to communicate ideas, listen actively, negotiate actions and resolve conflicts. Each student must contribute a section of the final report and in so doing demonstrate both his or her understanding of the report genre and general written expression skills. Similarly, students must contribute to their team's oral presentation, an activity that requires skills in public speaking. Through their participation in this topic, students learn that communication is an integral part of an engineer's professional duties.

Simultaneously with their team project work, students attend Language in Use classes. Language in Use is a course component in which written and oral communication skills relevant to project work are explicitly taught and practised. The course covers such aspects as meeting procedure, report structure, public speaking, correspondence and reading strategies. The emphasis is on clear, correct and effective communication. Languages in Use teachers also operate as test readers, giving detailed feedback on students' reports at the draft stage.

Use of expert teachers

Engineering academics, regardless of their personal level of communications skills, are not trained to teach communications topics. Recognizing this, the school of engineering has drawn on expertise available elsewhere within the university.

Teachers for the Language in Use component are drawn from the Flinders University Study Skills Centre. Staff members of the Study Skills Centre are academics with expertise in the use of English for academic purposes. Their work involves a mixture of academic counselling, running specific study skills workshops and teaching in a range of courses. Several of the staff are trained in teaching English as a second language.

Collaborating with academics in particular subject areas has been an effective mode of operating for the centre. The engineering faculty has assisted this process by being clear about its course objectives. In the process, centre staff have developed further their ability to adapt teaching strategies and materials to the demands of a specific subject area.

Students' attitudes to communication skills

There are a number of reasons to expect that students who select engineering may have misgivings about the study of written and oral communication. One factor in students' attitudes relates to educational history. Engineering students have often taken a mathematics/science path through the secondary school system. English is not compulsory at senior secondary level in South Australia. Even though all students' literacy skills are assessed in the final year (through the Writing Based Literacy Assessment) it is still possible for a student to complete a school certificate with a minimal requirement of sustained prose writing. An example is the student who, in an initial self-assessment, wrote:

'My writing skills are poor as in the past three years I avoided English as a subject in the school. I was very happy to do scientific subjects even though they were much harder than other ones.'

The prospect of writing a report chapter may seem daunting to such a student.

Oral language skills have not traditionally been considered necessary for success in secondary school mathematics and sciences courses. Students may thus be surprised, and even dismayed, to find their public speaking skills assessed as part of an engineering course. When students in this writer's class were asked to describe their abilities in the four topic components (reading, writing, teamwork and speaking), it was speaking that most students highlighted as a disliked or weak area. One student expressed his attitude thus:

'I despise public speaking. In some situations it is acceptable but in useless classroom exercises it can become monotonous . . . I can say that I am not too crash-hot at public speaking.'

Another, related, factor in student attitudes is gender. Engineering students are much more likely to be male than female. Males are more likely to occupy the lowest band for achievement in subject English and less likely to occupy the highest band than females (Alloway and Gilbert, 1997; NSW GACETT, 1994). Male school students reportedly see subject English as 'irrelevant' and 'boring'

(Martino, 1994) and these attitudes persist well after school years are over (Nichols, 1994).

Of course, not all male students have avoided subject English and even if they have, this does not mean they cannot cope with tertiary literacy. However, in order for students to take up the offered opportunity to improve their communication skills, Language in Use teachers must be ready to overcome any negative perceptions. It is important that the curriculum is tailored to the students' primary interest (engineering) so that its relevance is obvious. It is also crucial that students whose school literacy background is not strong be given explicit teaching in skills and plenty of opportunity to practise.

LANGUAGE IN USE CURRICULUM

The Language in Use curriculum is designed to run alongside and support the students' project work. There are three major components: project process, report writing, and oral presentation.

Project process

In their Language in Use classes, students have the opportunity to learn and practise the written and oral communication skills they will need in order to be an effective member of a project team. Early in the course, formal meeting procedure is introduced and students experience the roles of team member, team leader and secretary.

Students are introduced to the range of forms of written communication used in professional situations: the formal letter, memo, fax and e-mail. One of their first assessed tasks is a letter seeking information from, or an appointment with, someone from industry. Their engineering project team leaders often provide contacts for students to access.

A group-oriented problem-solving approach is also used in the teaching of the other course components, report writing and oral presentation.

Report writing

Students are taken through the structure of the report in detail. Teaching points include: how to write effective abstracts, introductions, bodies and conclusions; how to develop a system of numbered headings and sub-headings; and how to use an appropriate professional written register. Students are shown models of good practice and given opportunities in class to develop these skills.

Researching a report requires students to find and process information that is often quite detailed and complex. Lecturers encourage students to be strategic and directed in their use of information. The skills of overviewing, skimming and summarizing are demonstrated and practised in class. Students are required to submit an article review and are assessed on their ability to accurately summarize and provide relevant commentary.

Referencing and in-text citation are also taught in class. Here the emphasis is on the practical purpose of acknowledging sources. Students are encouraged to think of themselves as members of a professional community and of referencing as a means of making sources of information available to others within this community.

Students submit their report chapters for assessment twice. A draft is submitted just before mid-semester break and lecturers give detailed feedback on structure, format, referencing and written expression. Viewing the drafts gives the lecturer an opportunity to assess how well the skills and knowledge taught in class are being applied in practice. Teaching in the second half of the module is then tailored to addressing specific areas of need in preparation for the final submission.

The teaching of the report writing component has been greatly assisted by a purpose-written book *Report Writing Style Guide for Engineering Students* (Winckel and Hart, 1996). This book was the product of a collaboration between the Faculty of Engineering and the Flexible Learning Centre of the University of South Australia.

Oral presentation

As part of their assessment for Team Project and Communication Skills, project groups are required to present their research findings in a seminar. Language in Use gives students the opportunity to learn and practise the skills of oral presentation that will assist them to participate successfully in their final group seminar.

Public speaking is initially introduced to students within the context of mounting an argument and students are given a structure within which to plan a short opinionative talk. The class is also given, or develops through discussion, some guidelines for appropriate audience behaviour. Lecturers give positive and constructive feedback and peer assessors are encouraged take a similar approach. This talk is done for practice only, not counted towards the course grade.

The second public speaking activity is done as a group and is an assessed and graded course component. Generally, groups have prepared a presentation related to their project topic. This talk gives students an opportunity to refine their public speaking skills prior to participating in their final seminar for Team Project. Prior to working on the talk, students view a video 'Be prepared to speak' and discuss the accompanying notes. The video reinforces lecturer teaching on public speaking and sets it in a professional context. The group presentations are assessed on talk structure, oral communication skills and teamwork by the lecturer and peers.

An alternative approach to the group presentation was successfully trialled in 1997 and has now been made an option for lecturers. In this alternative activity, groups are asked to prepare a presentation promoting an engineering service or product. The preparation process involves: selecting a product/service, producing a draft written description, seeking and giving feedback on groups' drafts, identifying a target audience, and writing a press release. The final presentation is assessed on the criteria outlined above, as well as the group's ability to engage with their identified target audience. The class imaginatively enters the role of target audience members for the purpose of the exercise.

Students have shown considerable creativity and initiative in developing and presenting their promotional talks. Many of the groups took a futuristic approach to the product they were promoting. One product, for instance, was the 'minimizing car', capable of shrinking to pocket size, described with a full 'scientific' explanation and demonstrated by sleight-of-hand.

Outcomes

Language in Use is primarily focused on the communication skills required for successful completion of the project task. Therefore, a fair measure of the success of this programme is the quality of the projects, as indicated by student grades. While the projects are team exercises, students are allocated individual grades based on their report chapters. The grades referred to here are those allocated by the Engineering teaching staff to the projects and thus reflect the perceptions of engineering professionals on the standard of the projects.

In 1997 a total of 64 students submitted projects. The average grade was 68.5 per cent which is in the credit band. Twenty-five students received a grade in the distinction band. Only three students failed the project component. So, according to the standards of the engineering profession, the students' projects were more than satisfactory. This indicates that the Language in Use curriculum has succeeded in its aim of facilitating the acquisition of discipline-relevant written and oral communication skills.

Information about student perceptions comes from a survey undertaken in 1993 and the student evaluation conducted for this writer's class in 1997. The 1993 survey was an attempt to gauge the effectiveness of what was then a new programme (Downing *et al*, 1993). The responses relate to the entire programme rather than just to the Language in Use component. Most respondents expressed the view that the subjects had 'improved their self-confidence as learners' (Downing et al, 1993). The survey authors also report that: 'Anecdotal evidence . . . strongly endorsed the importance of the social interaction that the participation in a team provided, in reducing the isolation many first-year students experience'.

The Student Evaluation of Teaching survey (SET) is used in South Australian universities to provide information about the quality of topics offered. The SET asks students to record their responses to questions about expectations of them, teaching methods and learning outcomes. In the SET completed by this writer's 1997 class of 17 students, all students agreed, or strongly agreed, that their understanding of communication had increased, that they felt positive about the topic and that their ability to work independently had increased. All agreed, or strongly agreed, that the materials were helpful and the assessment was fair.

When asked whether the topic's aims had been met, 11 were in agreement; however six were undecided. This perhaps reflects the fact that the aims of the

Language in Use module are to support student work in another topic, Team Project. However it also suggests that the topic's aims need to be more clearly stated and reinforced by teachers.

Students were also asked to nominate the best aspect of the topic. The most popular response was the public speaking element. In the initial self-assessments, public speaking featured as the aspect of the curriculum in which students felt least confidence. Other positive comments related to the feedback given on students' written work and the one-to-one attention available. Criticism was limited. Two students commented on the timing of deadlines and one felt the class size was too large.

It appears that gains from the programme are enduring ones. Since the first-year course was changed to include the integrated project and communications curriculum, the standard of final year projects has been high, according to head of the school, Andrew Downing. The combined professional engineering societies of Australia hold an annual 'Student Papers' night, awarding prizes to the best presentations. Last year, Flinders students were awarded first and second prizes. Presentations by undergraduate students at national conferences are becoming quite a regular event.

Overall, Language in Use is fulfilling the engineering school's aims of improving the written and oral communication skills of all its students in the critical first-year period and of providing a sound foundation for students' future professional lives.

Communication skills can be taught effectively to engineering students if the communication component of the curriculum is closely linked to the engineering component. The key mechanism for achieving this link is the team project. The project task is constructed in such a way that a range of communication skills is needed for successful completion. Language in Use provides students with the opportunity to acquire and practise these skills with the guidance of expert staff. My experience as a Language in Use teacher is that students are strongly motivated to succeed in the team project and as a result are open to learning the skills required.

Within the Language in Use curriculum, the following factors contribute to effective teaching and learning:

- explicit teaching and modelling of all skills;

- provision of opportunities to practise newly acquired skills;

- provision of feedback at formative stages of tasks (eg at the draft chapter stage);

- use of group work activities that mirror the project team process;

- use of discipline-relevant examples and readings;

- close monitoring of students with literacy difficulties and referral to further support if necessary.

While teaching is done separately, collaboration between engineering and study skills staff is essential to achieve consistency. The school of engineering assists this process by being explicit about its requirements. As mentioned above, the project report guidelines are comprehensively described in a purpose-commissioned text (Winckel and Hart, 1996).

It is also important that the reports, which are the culmination of the semester's work, are not only well written but professionally presented. The Engineering School carries the cost of printing of project reports so that students can be assured of a professionally presented product. Seeing the reports produced by the previous year's cohort inspires each new class of students.

Finally, student motivation is increased by knowing that their projects will be published to a professional audience, that is the team leaders who are drawn from the engineering industry. While students appreciate the feedback of the Language in Use teachers, the real arbiters of the success of the project are their professional role models. In this way, we are truly preparing students for their future as articulate and literate engineers.

Acknowledgements

Thanks to Professor Andrew Downing and Sue Roberts for their helpful comments. Thanks to Ed Irons who played a vital role in making the Language in Use course what it is.

REFERENCES

Alloway, N and Gilbert, P (1997) Everything is dangerous: Working with boys in literacy classrooms, paper presented at the 1st Joint National Conference of the AATE, ALEA and ASLA, Darwin, July

Downing, AR *et al* (1993) Engineering systems: An integrated project and communications based introduction to engineering, Australasian Association of Engineering Education, Proceedings 5th Annual Convention and Conference, pp. 39–44, Auckland, 12–15 December 1993

Hadgraft, R (1993) A problem-based approach to civil engineering education, in *Research and Development in Problem-Based Learning*, vol 1, ed G Ryan, Australian Problem Based Learning Network, Campbelltown, NSW

Harrington, DP (1996) Why bad things happen to good clinical engineers, *Journal of Clinical Engineering*, **21** (2), pp 105–7

Hessami, MA and Gani, R (1993) Using problem-based learning in the mechanical engineering degree, in *Research and Development in Problem-Based Learning*, vol 1, ed G Ryan, Australian Problem Based Learning Network, Campbelltown, NSW

Martino, W (1994) Masculinity and learning: Exploring boys' underachievement and under-representation in subject English, *Interpretations*, **27** (2), August, pp 22–57

Nichols, S (1994) Fathers and Literacy, *Australian Journal of Language and Literacy*

NSW GACETT (New South Wales Government Advisory Committee on Education, Training and Tourism) (1994) Challenges and opportunities: a discussion paper, NSW Department of School Education, Sydney

Robinson, CM and Blair, GM (1995) Writing skills training for engineering students in large classes, *Higher Education*, **30**, pp 99–114

Spencer, M (1998) Employers lament inability to write, *The Australian*, higher education section, p 37, 24 June

Van Driel, J *et al* (1997) Teachers' craft knowledge and curriculum innovation in higher engineering education, *Higher Education*, **34**, pp 105–22

Winckel, A and Hart, B (1996) *Report Writing Style Guide for Engineering Students*, Faculty of Engineering and Flexible Learning Centre, University of South Australia

10

Library and Information Skills for the Reluctant Student

Carol Primrose

SUMMARY

Developments in bibliographic databases over the last 20 years or so have radically changed the skills required of students at all levels for successful information retrieval. Unfortunately, students have not kept up with these developments and tend to be unaware of the need for knowledge of the basic techniques for electronic search strategy, using Boolean logic and other options.

Students also find it difficult to accept that these skills apply to all bibliographic databases and that therefore there is no need for instruction to be subject-specific except within very broad areas.

To change these attitudes, the library at The University of Glasgow developed a suite of interactive computer-assisted learning packages, which were then evaluated both internally and externally. Feedback from librarians and students has been enthusiastic. They can be used at any time by individual students on the library's network, but they have also been incorporated into teaching programmes.

One of the packages, 'Computer Sources', is described in some detail, as is its role in the development of information skills training in The University of Glasgow. The Arts and Divinity Research Training Course is briefly described as an example.

INTRODUCTION

Readers of this volume may be a little surprised to find the inclusion of a paper from a librarian. What 'subject' do librarians teach? In fact, academic librarians often find themselves with a considerable teaching load introducing users to electronic information retrieval. Indeed, it is not unusual for their 'pupils' to include academic staff as well as first year students, and postgraduate research level students. It is not unusual either for many students to fail to see the necessity for this tuition at the time it is offered.

BACKGROUND

Traditionally, the main form of undergraduate teaching in the older universities has generally been a course of lectures supplemented by written work based on a reading list or essay list. In terms of information retrieval this required little skill from the students where there were sufficient copies of books on the list to meet the demand. In recent years, things have changed. Not only is there insufficient funding to provide enough copies of recommended material, but in many subjects teaching methods have altered; in medicine, for example, right from the beginning of first year the curriculum requires students to work in teams to solve problems. Not the least of these problems is to locate and evaluate the relevant published work. In other subject areas, such skills may be called for at third-year level.

This kind of information retrieval by subject has been possible for many years using printed sources: classified library catalogues for books and abstracting and indexing journals for periodical literature. In general, the organizing principle of these sources is classified with a keyword index or alphabetically by keyword, but in each case only very simple, single-concept searches could be done and users generally coped well on their own. Beginning in the 1960s, however, both these types of sources started to appear in electronic form. At first, the high cost of searching remote dial-up databases meant that only library subject specialists were allowed to carry out searches, but developments in hardware and software, and the spread of networking, meant that end-users were gradually enabled to do their own searching. Today, virtually every academic library and the national libraries in this country and abroad have electronic catalogues, and there are scores of electronic databases of periodical literature, grey literature, patents, theses and other published material.

PROBLEMS ASSOCIATED WITH ELECTRONIC INFORMATION RETRIEVAL

Users

This development poses the user two problems. The first is simply the technical expertise needed to manipulate the hardware and operating software. In early days, library staff spent a lot of time teaching users the principles of keyboarding, mouse management and so on. Today, most students are highly competent in these areas, but there are still many mature and foreign students who need help. Such students often lack confidence or feel embarrassed at revealing their weakness.

The other problem is less self-evident. A computerized database offers the possibility of a very sophisticated and comprehensive search tightly focused on a narrow subject area, but only if the searcher is familiar with the principles of Boolean searching[1] which underlie all bibliographic databases and the additional features offered by individual databases. Students used to the Internet need a lot of convincing that they do not have these skills. The Internet itself is also a difficulty. It is haphazard, unregulated and very difficult to evaluate, exceedingly questionable as an information source, yet many students do not want to look beyond it.

Librarians

The problems for the librarian are partly logistic, partly psychological. It is quite difficult to persuade academic departments to release precious space in the lecture curriculum for a session on information skills. Without the academic respectability endowed by a place in the list of lectures it is very difficult to persuade students to attend for information skills training. Even when a lecture slot is made available, it is usually right at the beginning of term before students have been made aware of the information requirements of the course. Only when they actually try it on their own do they realize the complexity involved and come seeking help in ones and twos. There are never enough staff to deal with all students individually at any time of year.

More advanced information teaching needs to be done in a computing laboratory. Lectures and demonstrations in the classroom at this level are a waste of time, students must get hands-on practice, but there is fierce competition for access to the teaching laboratories. In the case of the major databases, there is a further complication in that the Internet is so congested in the afternoons that classes have to be scheduled in early evening, a further disincentive for some.

Nature of the material

Assuming the logistical problems can be overcome, that leaves the difficulty of the nature of the material being taught. Many students believe they can handle anything a computer throws at them, but no amount of computer games prepares students for information retrieval, and while 'surfing the net' is more effective if done with a well-thought-out search strategy, the 'net' does not help very much to develop the skills needed. A good strategy requires analysis of the topic, identification of the key concepts and the best terminology to describe them, identification of the relationships of the concepts and the expression of those relationships using Boolean logic[1] and any other devices offered by the database, such as truncation[2] and adjacency[3]. The sudden fall from thinking they know it all to being asked to learn something horribly technical that seems to involve algebra can be very demoralizing.

The questions addressed by this book: 'Why should I learn this? What's it got to do with chemistry/politics/Shakespearean tragedy?', also arise in the library. Users always want a database specific to their subject area; very often, there is no such thing. Databases on specific types of material, such as dissertation abstracts, are general, not subject specific. Many general databases are very important, because they contain tangential material that would not be found in a subject-specific list. Many search topics are cross-disciplinary and cannot be adequately covered in a single database. For these reasons, and for economy of production, teaching materials are not subject specific. The basic skills of Boolean searching are generic, they can be applied to every database; specific databases differ only in the symbols used to indicate Boolean relationships and the number of additional features available.

AN ELECTRONIC REMEDY: TEACHING AND LEARNING TECHNOLOGY IN THE UNIVERSITY OF GLASGOW

Fortunately, it was this very generic nature of information skills that allowed The University of Glasgow library to tap into the TLTP (Teaching and Learning Technology Programme) initiative in order to address some of our difficulties. This was a programme established jointly by the Higher Education Funding Councils of England, Scotland, Wales and Northern Ireland to encourage the development and integration of educational courseware. In the first three-year phase, The University of Glasgow was one of 43 projects funded.

The University of Glasgow is the second oldest in Scotland, founded in 1451, and one of the largest in the United Kingdom with 17,000 students, of whom around 3000 are from overseas. The university has nine faculties, including divinity and veterinary medicine, and offers courses in a huge range of subjects, some of which are taught by distance learning. The library has around one and a half million volumes, 7,000 periodical subscriptions, music recordings and scores, and many electronic databases. It is a European Documentation Centre, and has a Special Collections Department containing material from Egyptian papyri up to the present, including the Whistler papers, the Scottish Theatre Archive and letters and papers from alumni such as Adam Smith and Lord Kelvin. Subject specialists liaise with academic departments, attending departmental meetings and boards of studies, advising on information provision for teaching and research and providing training in information retrieval where required.

The University of Glasgow's TLTP project was known as TILT (Teaching with Independent Learning Technology). The project involved 19 departments including the library, and had as its objective the production of computer-assisted learning packages which would be incorporated into the teaching framework and encourage students to take more control over their own learning. The TILT project included an evaluation group that dealt with internal evaluation; additionally, the library's packages were reviewed or evaluated externally in other university libraries. One of the requirements of the TLTP programme was that materials should not be institution-specific but capable of being used throughout the higher education sector. This fitted perfectly with the production of information retrieval teaching packages since very few bibliographic databases are institution specific. Even library catalogues are based on shared software.

INTERACTIVE COMPUTER-ASSISTED LEARNING PACKAGES

The University of Glasgow library produced a suite of five packages on different aspects of information skills, including study skills in general. This paper will concentrate on one of them, 'Computer Sources', but here is a brief description of the others. The first package was aimed at the 'foolish virgins' in the first year who get to the library too late for any of the books on the reading list. 'Choosing Books and Journals' gives pointers to identifying other books in the subject area which are relevant, up to date and academically respectable, and includes some hints on reading techniques and note-taking. Two packages, one general, one on business information, were adapted from work done in The Robert Gordon University, Aberdeen, by Joan Robertson (Robertson, 1994). These tackle the first and most important skill in information retrieval which is to analyse the topic, identify the key concepts and discover the best terms to use to describe them. 'Study Skills' is a brief introduction to time management, lectures and note-taking, reading, writing, presentation, revision and examination techniques.

Computer Sources

Probably the most generally useful package is Computer Sources. The design idea is that of a treasure hunt that most students find quite entertaining, though one or two thought it beneath their dignity. Examples are given in a mock-up of a general database similar to BIDS (Bath International Data Service, Citation Index) so that users get something of the feel of a live search. The packages are intended to be generic so they are not open to major restructuring, but in this one some examples, such as lists of databases, are in text files which can be customized to reflect the circumstances of individual institutions.

The package is in three sections: basic principles, advanced methods and practical exercises.

Basic principles

The basic section has five subsections:

1. What are computer sources? gives an overview of what computer sources are in terms of bibliographic information. Some list books, some give details of journal articles, sometimes with a brief abstract of the contents, and some give the full text of the article. CD ROM and on-line formats are considered with examples of each.

2. Find the right starting point. The key is to know the subject; students are pointed towards reference sources which will give them an overview of the subject and the terminology. With this they can identify the themes and keywords they need; then they need to think of synonyms and related terms, not forgetting variant spellings, eg English and American, where appropriate, to come up with their search terms. Examples given are pollution/ acid rain/effluent/toxic waste and labor/labour.

3. Plan your route. This looks at keyword searching using a single word or phrase with truncation, that is, using a symbol such as * or ? (depending on the database) at the end of a word to make the search include variants

such as singulars and plurals. It includes a warning against truncating too early; for example to truncate engineering you should not use eng* or you will get very many 'false hits' such as England and English. These keywords can then be combined using Boolean terms AND, OR and NOT. The effect of each is illustrated using Venn diagrams. Some databases use the words themselves to indicate the relationships, others use symbols, eg BIDS uses plus (+) for AND, the comma (,) for OR and the dash(-) for NOT. This section also covers field searching which allows a search by specific details, eg author's name, journal title, year of publication, language, document type, etc.

4. Your goal is in sight. Once run, a search should be checked to see how many relevant references it has retrieved, and refined if necessary; if too few, add synonyms linked by OR, and truncation; if too many, add more terms linked by AND and NOT, or limit by field.

5. How to take home the prize. Mark relevant references and note for future use by printing, e-mailing or downloading them to a floppy disk.

This section closes with a summary of the above.

Advanced methods

Advanced Methods has four subsections:

1. Keyword searching. This looks at more complex Boolean searches including nesting (use of parentheses to link concepts), and adjacency (the specification of the order and distance apart of words in a phrase). Examples are:

   (mammal or bird*) and (sea or marine or ocean)* and PY=1990–1994 – this search is using truncation, nesting, Boolean AND and OR, and a five-year range limit for date of publication.

   recall/1/hypnosis – finds recall under hypnosis, etc without slowing the search by including a very common word.

2. Controlled vocabulary. Databases frequently restrict the choice of terminology by using a thesaurus, which users need to consult to find the correct term. These are often American, for example: *community health* must be replaced by *public health service*, *public toilets* become *public comfort stations*. Indexes should also be consulted to check the form or spelling of an author's name.

3. Cited reference searching. Citation indexes allow users to work forward from a known reference, by locating all later published work which includes that reference in the list of references. It is possible to trace the influence of a seminal paper by this means.

4 . General search tips. Documentation provided by the library, and help screens, should not be ignored.

Practical exercises

The practical exercises have four questions asking users to identify synonyms, and another four asking them to choose the most successful search statement of three or four alternatives. In addition, some research topics are given for analysis:

- What are the mechanisms involved in the memory of mammals?

- Account for the rise in popularity of opera in Britain in the last decade.

- How do viruses avoid the immune system and establish chronic infection?

TECHNICAL SPECIFICATIONS

The platform chosen for all the packages was PC since this was rapidly becoming the standard in the university at the time we set out; the minimum specification is a 386 machine with VGA graphics facility. The software chosen was originally 'Guide' for its text-handling capabilities, but as the programme progressed we developed a style which used relatively little text and much more in the way of graphics and interactive hypertext and consequently switched to 'Toolbook'. This had the advantage of allowing us to include a runtime version in the package so potential users did not have to buy their own copies of the full software.

All the packages are highly interactive with examples and exercises to reinforce the message. They all have a common format with a menu bar with menu, forward, back and exit options appearing at the foot of each screen, and a tutorial on using the mouse at the beginning (which can be skipped if inappropriate), so that even comparatively inexperienced users can move round the package with confidence. The exercise option gives feedback so that the user can judge his or her progress and, where they have gone wrong, get information as to what the error was and what the right answer is. In the floppy disk format, there is a notepad facility so that students can make their own notes, but most packages include a summary that the user can also download. Each has a modular format which means that the user can take the component sections in any order, or skip sections which are already familiar. Library Search Skills, Computer Sources and Study Skills are now also available in a WWW format.

EVALUATION OF THE PACKAGES

Evaluation was built into the TILT programme from the beginning and these packages were evaluated in-house by the evaluation group. The evaluation team selects from some 15 measures including pre- and post-intervention questionnaires, observations of students interacting with the package, semi-structured interviews and a confidence log. On the basis of their responses to such measures we were able to obtain students' views on the package, both ease of use and value of content. We also tried to establish learning outcomes but this is very difficult with generic skills.

One large-scale evaluation attempt on Choosing Books and Journals with *c*150 summer-school students was vitiated to some degree by technical problems in one computing laboratory and the logistics of getting that number in and out of laboratories and library stacks, but overall the exercise suggested that students did learn from it. The students were divided into two groups: the first group was given the task of finding information in the library first, the other worked on the package; halfway through the exercise they changed over. Very few of the students needed help to operate the package and confidence in their ability to perform the required task increased steadily. Half of them said they would use the package again, the other half felt they had gained all they needed on the first run through. Allowing for the problems such large numbers had actually getting to terminals and into stacks, the answer papers suggested that about 75 per cent tackled the problems successfully. Given that only 50 per cent claimed to have had any previous library instruction and about 70 per cent used a library only once a month or less, this suggests that they had learned some skills.

Computer Sources was evaluated by smaller groups of undergraduates and postgraduates. These students were all practised computer users, but most agreed that they had learned from the package. All but one said they would recommend it to others.

Because the library's contribution to the TILT programme was entirely in-house, unlike some other departments which were cooperating with other universities, we felt it necessary to canvass some external opinions. Packages were reviewed by Nicholas Bowskill, TLTP Project IT in Teaching and Learning, School of Education, University of Durham; by Barbara Middleton, Assistant Librarian (IT and Liaison), the Robinson Library, University of Newcastle; by Rob Duffin, Research Associate, University of Sheffield; by Patrick Teskey, Sub-Librarian, University of Ulster; and by Ian Cantley, Computing Officer, Educational Services, University of Ulster (Creanor et al, 1995). Overall, response was highly favourable, despite minor complaints, with particular mention of the graphics and design, animation, computer-simulations and feedback.

A larger-scale evaluation of Computer Sources was carried out in the University of Southampton, thanks to Oren Stone and the Hartley Library, involving 74 students, including some non-native English speakers in an induction programme in the Language Centre. The questionnaire returns indicated that the vast majority found the package informative and easy to use and most felt the material was at the right level. Students would have liked more examples and details of particular databases; they liked its simplicity of use, the examples and exercises and the graphics; one felt it would be improved if we 'covered all the sources all over the world' (Creanor *et al*, 1995: 62). Clearly, you can't please all of the people all of the time. In fact this desire for more on particular databases was a little depressing, since one of the objects of the package was to demonstrate that most of the skills you need for database searching are transferable from one to another.

SUPPLEMENTARY MATERIALS

In the arts faculty we have supplemented the package with Workbooks on three major databases, BIDS Arts and Humanities Citation Index, OCLC FirstSearch and EDINA Periodicals Contents Index, to meet this need. During the Arts and Divinity Research Training Course students undertake 12 hours of IT[4] (basics, word-processing, graphics, Internet, etc), six hours of library skills, and two hours of research methodology.

The library module comprises one two-hour lecture covering an introduction to library facilities, Boolean logic and search strategy, record keeping, citing references and compiling the bibliography; this was followed by two laboratory sessions looking at Computer Sources. Students then go on-line to search BIDS and OCLC using the workbooks provided, which are designed to take them through all the most important features of each database. For the purpose of assessment, students are asked to download certain items retrieved via the databases, translate the data into an accepted bibliographic form (author-title or author-date) and house style (Harvard, MLA, Vancouver, etc), and then present it in the form of a bibliography. This course, and those of the other faculties that have been developed, is compulsory and has its own external examiner, so both students and staff take it seriously.

CONCLUSION

The University of Glasgow library's TILT project is now finished, but the results are still proving useful. Well over 500 copies of the packages have been sold to institutions worldwide. At home, the packages are available on the university network and on that of the Clyde Virtual University metropolitan area, so students can access it at will. Since we started out, the library has been endowed with a considerable number of new high-specification personal computers for student use and the number of computing laboratories has increased, so access is easier. Computer Sources is an integral part of the undergraduate IT programme's module on information retrieval, and it is used as backup for the postgraduate research training courses. The teaching of such skills in this way is also beginning to be adopted in some honours' courses and demand looks set to increase steadily. So, the librarian's Cinderella subject is getting invited to the ball, thanks in no small measure to the work done with TILT.

NOTES

1. Boolean logic is the principle used by bibliographic database software that enables the specification of relationships between search terms in order to focus a search more tightly. The Boolean concepts are AND, OR and NOT. For examples, see the section in Appendix 10.1 on Refining Searches, Boolean Operators.

2.   Truncation is the mechanism whereby the database will find all terms beginning or ending with the letters specified by the searcher. For examples, see the section in Appendix 10.1 on Refining Searches, Truncation. Most databases offer right-hand truncation allowing variation in the ends of words, a few offer left-hand truncation allowing variation in the beginnings of words. Occasionally a database allows 'wild card' searching which allows variation in the middle of words, eg wom?n.

3.   Adjacency allows searching for two or more terms which may be up to a given number of words apart from each other in a journal title or abstract, eg liver/2/cancer would find liver cancer and cancer of the liver. Sometimes it is also possible to specify the order in which words must appear.

4.   IT – information technology. In this context it refers to a standard module of instruction in basic computer skills for academic researchers, not to computing science.

REFERENCES

Creanor, L *et al* (1995) A hypertext approach to information skills: Development and evaluation, a report by the University of Glasgow's institutional project in the Teaching and Learning Technology Programme Teaching with Independent Learning Technologies, University of Glasgow, Glasgow
Robertson, J (1994) Information skills in further education: a hypertext approach to learning in business studies, PhD thesis, The Robert Gordon University, Aberdeen

APPENDIX 10.1 ARTS AND DIVINITY RESEARCH TRAINING COURSE

The University of Glasgow library bids worksheet

Keyword or subject searching

SINGLE WORD

Choose **Words in title**, **keywords** or **abstract** from the Search menu by typing no 2 and pressing return.
Type in *Byzantium* and press Return.
The top of the screen shows the number of **HITS** (references found).
How many are there?
Display the list of hits by, first, typing **D** and Return.
Then select the level of detail required from the Display menu.
For now, choose **Titles only** by typing no 1 and Return.
Scroll through the list using the **down arrow key**. Notice that an **arrow** appears

at the left-hand side of the record at the top of the screen, and the **number** of that record shows in the **Status Bar** above.

Look for the title *Byzantium and its army*; bring it to the top of the screen, and note its number.

Select it by typing **D** and Return, then select **Full Record** by typing 4 and Return, then type the record number and Return.

Notice the **Field Indicators** (**AU**, **TI**, etc)

What kind of document is this item?

MARK this record.

E-mail the results to yourself.

REFINING SEARCHES

Truncation

You can look for words with variant endings, eg singular and plural forms, by truncating with the sign (*).

Look for *Scotland*. How many hits?

Look for *Scottish*. How many hits?

Look for *Scot**. How many hits?

Truncating can result in very large lists. It is sometimes better to use the Boolean operator **'OR'**, see below.

Boolean operators: 'AND', 'OR', 'NOT'.

These enable you to combine terms in a number of ways.

AND – the system will look for the search terms in any order. Each record found will contain all the search terms. It usually decreases the number of hits. 'AND' is indicated by the plus sign (+).

Look for *roman + pottery*. How many hits?

Look for *roman + pottery + amphora**. How many hits?

OR – the system will look for the search terms in any order. Each record found need contain only one of the search terms. It usually increases the number of hits.

'OR' is indicated by the comma (,).

Look for *scotland, scottish*. How many hits?

But note that this is more precise than truncation in this instance, see *Scot** above.

NOT – is used to exclude one aspect of a topic, eg *poetry not epic*. In general it is not very helpful in arts areas.

'NOT' is indicated by the hyphen sign (-).

NB: it is important to **LINK** the concepts correctly.

Look for *roman + pottery, amphora**. How many hits?

Look for *roman* + (*pottery, amphora**) How many hits?
The system is interpreting the first version as (*roman* + *pottery*) or (*amphora**),
not as (*roman pottery*) or (*roman amphora*).

NB: for arts subjects it is often more effective to do a number of separate
searches on fairly simple search terms, than to try to construct one very elaborate
one.

AUTHOR SEARCHING

Look for *Hendel_RS*.
Display the list of hits. Find and display full record for *Notes on the Greek Text of
Genesis*. Mark this record.

JOURNALS

1. To find an **article** published in a particular journal.
Choose Search then menu no 4.
The screen then offers you the choice of a keyword **Journal title expression**
or an **exact journal** title search.
Choose Journal title expression. Look for *Antiquity*. How many hits?
Go back to search screen, etc. and choose exact title. Look for *Antiquity*. Display
hits. Give the full citation for the first record.

2. To see the **contents** of a particular issue of a journal.
Choose **Issues** by typing I, then from the menu you can choose to specify a
particular issue, or look at the latest issue.

LIMITS

Choose **Options**. Select the **Year range**. Press return.
Change both dates to 1994 by overtyping. Use the right-hand arrow key or the
tab key to go to the second box. Press return. Choose Search.
Look for *Viking**. How many hits?
Give the author of the 4th record.
Choose **Options**. Change dates to 1981–1995. Choose **Options** again.
Select **Language**. Change to **Danish** only – scroll list until it is at the top and
mark it by pressing spacebar. Then press Q. Choose search.
Look for *Viking**. How many hits?
Reset dates to 1994–1996. **Reset** language to **English**.
Select **Document** type. Choose journal article.
Choose Search. Look for *Byzantium*.
Who went 'sailing to Byzantium'?

11

Communication Skills Using Legal, Ethical and Professional Issues

AC Lynn Zelmer

SUMMARY

This chapter deals with the need to improve the communications skills of graduates. The example focuses on information technology (IT) graduates, for whom prospective employers have demanded improved communication capabilities. Although discussed here within the context of IT graduates, the issue is one faced in all disciplines.

The Human Issues in Computing (HIC) unit was developed because an existing communications unit was universally disliked by staff and students, and the IT industry demanded improved communication skills among IT graduates.

HIC successfully introduces communication and groupwork skills for on-campus and distance students in the context of the legal, ethical and professional issues common to the IT industry in which the students will be seeking employment.

The author describes how IT (with which his students are very familiar) can be utilized, support and enhance learning.

INTRODUCTION

HIC is a required first-year unit in the three-year Bachelor of Information Technology (BInfoTech) degree at Australia's Central Queensland University (CQU). This applied computing programme is offered to school leavers at campus locations and mature students at a distance, resulting in a wide range of backgrounds and motivations.

In the early 1990s the Australian Computer Society, government and industry groups were demanding improved communication and related skills for IT graduates. Universities were graduating 'technonerds' who had excellent computing skills but who lacked the corresponding abilities to work in teams or to communicate effectively. At CQU, staff and students universally disliked the required communications unit. The author responded by developing a new unit, HIC, which also provided students with an introduction to the legal, ethical and professional issues they would encounter as IT professionals.

The institution

CQU now has over 10,000 students, five regional campuses for Australian students, three capital city campuses for international students studying in Australia, an international campus in Fiji, and study centres in three other Asian countries. Students studying at a distance, often mature students who continue to work while they study, have long been a major component of the student body.

Until about five years ago, CQU's distance education materials were developed by staff lecturing in the same unit on a Queensland regional campus and were mostly print-based with some audiotape or videotape supplementation. The resulting teaching materials were costly to prepare or revise and did not cater to the unique needs of the distance or international students. Although some unit developers have used teleconferencing, video conferencing, and computer-based delivery to supplement or replace conventional paper-based materials, it is the existence of these materials which has enabled the recent campus expansion.

CQU faculties were restructured in 1998 to put together similar programmes, enabling staff and students to build on shared values and facilities. The unit described in this paper is offered through the Faculty of Informatics and Communications, which has undergraduate and postgraduate programmes in communications, electronic journalism, information systems, information technology, health informatics, and mathematics. The university hopes that this combination of communications and technology applications will be more attractive to students, particularly female students, than more conventional structures.

The course and unit

The BInfoTech is a three-year professional degree in applied computing with software engineering and systems services streams. Graduates receive Australian Computer Society Level One accreditation.

One of the driving forces behind the evolution of the BInfoTech was a 1992 discipline review of the communication and teamwork skills of typical IT graduates. 'The Review hit us with our students being competent with technology – as well accepted as technonerds – but absolutely abysmal communicators.' (Zelmer in Lincoln, 1995: 27)

Students had had a required communications unit in their programme. Technical and Professional Communications (Tech & Prof Comm) was a service unit developed by the Faculty of Arts for delivery to a wide variety of science and engineering students. Students completed a series of generic assignments that emphasized communication theory, writing style and grammar. Grading was on a combination of assignment marks, 'class participation', and a final examination. The materials used for 'teaching' the unit at a distance had been developed from the classroom lectures and thus were inappropriate for many students studying independently.

With all of these faults, Tech & Prof Comm might still have been a viable unit for the IT students if it had been more practical and had allowed the students to focus on topics and issues relevant to their personal or professional interests. Practical politics in the institution, however, meant that it was easier to develop a new discipline-specific unit.

HIC is a required unit for all students in the BInfoTech. Learning occurs through the use of videotaped lectures and other study resources organized around three required assignments. Aside from the videotaped lectures, almost all the study materials are delivered electronically. These materials can be accessed using a Web browser from the class Web site, from the diskettes provided to distance students, or from files downloaded to their own hard drive.

Since the unit uses IT to teach IT, the first task for most students is to print a copy of the unit profile and assignment details. However, students are discouraged from printing out the whole collection of resource materials (roughly 200 pages). Instead they are encouraged to read the materials from their computer screen to get them used to using on-line documentation.

Support services include e-mail, telephone and fax plus direct contact with the author by telephone or an e-mail discussion list. With roughly 600 students in the unit, annually the lecturer spends an average of one hour per day answering e-mail queries. Students studying on a campus also have local tutors available for individual and group assistance.

On successful completion of the unit students should know where to find information and assistance on legal, ethical, and professional issues likely to confront the IT professional; know where to find information and assistance on tasks such as writing a technical report or making a presentation to a small group; and be able to apply this knowledge and skills at a level appropriate for a first-year IT student.

HUMAN ISSUES IN COMPUTING: THE FIRST ITERATION

The entry standards and reading level of our IT students have frequently been questioned and it is generally agreed that their writing skills are often inadequate by any professional standard. As a result they often avoid written assignments, a problem when second- and third-year students are required to prepare reports on software development projects and other activities. On the other hand, IT students are generally very interested in professional IT issues, such as data privacy or software theft. They will spend hours exchanging messages on such topics in a news group or on-line chat room.

The initial HIC offering had three main objectives:

- ensure that all students meet a basic level of communication and groupwork skills;

- introduce students to the variety of legal, ethical and other issues they will encounter in their professional work;

- encourage students to be self-motivated and self-managed, skills that should be useful in later years as IT professionals.

Unit development was constrained by resource limitations; however, it was agreed that the unit was to be developed with the needs of distance students as the primary focus, a first for the faculty.

Videotaped lectures and interviews with guest speakers from the IT industry provided the core materials for the unit. Copies of the tapes were available in campus libraries for students who missed the classroom viewing session and students studying at a distance received the tapes for personal viewing. The author visited classes on the three campuses where the unit was first offered at least twice during the term (either in person or via teleconference) and an academic staff member was available on each campus for liaison and student support. As well, all students had mail, telephone, e-mail and fax contact for answering their queries.

Other resource materials for this initial offering were print-based. One resource booklet included advice for computer novices on copying and backing up files, connecting to the university computer system, sending e-mail and other technical topics. Another was a (hopefully inspirational) collection of current newspaper and journal articles highlighting current legal, ethical and professional issues as reported in the national press.

The unit was based around eight practical IT assignments that could be submitted in any order or at any time during the term using any computer system available to the student. A detailed outline was provided for each reporting activity to ensure an appropriate report format and style.

The initial offering of the new unit met with mixed reactions among the staff and 300 students on-campus and at a distance, although overall the students were pleased with the relevance of the unit's content.

- Some staff were unhappy that students were attending on-campus classes without a lecturer being present, even though each class had a designated student responsible for the management of the class. Few of the campus-based students were happy about the lack of a lecturer at every class; most avoided the opportunity to be the designated student responsible for a class session. Complaints ceased when a tutor/demonstrator was provided for every on-campus class in subsequent offerings.

- Most students were pleased with the videotaped lectures and were particularly pleased with the ability to view the weekly lecture at another time if they had missed a class.

- Mature students were very happy with assignments that allowed them to report on their professional work and explore issues relevant to their daily activities.

- A small but significant number of students were pleased with the flexibility provided by assignments that could be completed at their own time and in any order; however, many students were unable to manage a study schedule which did not have fixed assignment submission dates, resulting in a high rate of non-submission. This was initially resolved by requiring students to submit assignments by a specific date, and later by restructuring the assignments.

- Those students using the e-mail and telephone support system were generally pleased with the support they received.

- The author was overwhelmed by the amount of work involved in providing e-mail and telephone support for both campus-based and distance students working on a variety of computer platforms.

EVOLUTION OF THE UNIT

This initial experience led to a number of changes within the unit, particularly to overcome the frustration level among some of the recent school-leavers who seem to need a high level of 'hand holding'. The changes occurred in parallel with several programmes to attract more female students and attempted to better accommodate their needs for flexible content delivery and assessment.

University restructuring has resulted in a reduction from 15 to 12 weeks in each term, and an expansion from two to four terms per year (two of the terms have a six-week format, one before and one after Christmas) to assist with students who wish to 'fast track' their degrees. Cost reduction measures have also reduced the number of time slots available for examinations, forestalling a push by the author's colleagues to introduce an examination for HIC. Students, incidentally, prefer units without examinations and have been highly supportive of the reduction of formal examination requirements.

HIC is currently offered at least three times per year and in both the six and twelve-week formats. Unlike most offerings from the faculty, the unit is only revised once per year, thus facilitating materials distribution and management of the unit. It also significantly reduces the author's development workload, allowing time for the roughly one hour per day required every working day of the year to answer students' e-mail and other queries. This individual and group contact provides the flexibility and customization that supposedly only comes from frequent unit revision.

Assignment and materials changes

Even without an examination, the initial offerings – eight competency-based assessment items – were ruled excessive for a first-year unit. They have been restructured into three multicomponent assignments with fixed submission dates. Detailed outlines (pro formas) are provided for all reports.

- Observe, and report on, a formal meeting of 6 to 20 people; verification required by the meeting chair or secretary; a text-based e-mail report is required in addition to the signed paper-based report.

- Research an IT-related moral, legal or ethical issue introduced in a range of supplied case studies, organize a discussion group and lead a discussion on the issue, and report on the results of the discussion; assessed on participant evaluation, report content and presentation. Suggested case discussion topics include cultural change, gender differences, plagiarism, copyright, privacy of data, techno-fear and health, and student access to the Internet.

- Install a new piece of software, learn its use and provide a novice user with at least two hours of instruction on the use of the software; student-prepared instructional materials required; an e-mail report with attachment in a specified format is required.

While the assignments have been designed so that experiences in one should assist in completing the next, many students do not see the connection. The 1999 materials are being modified to make these connections more explicit.

Previously paper-based materials are now provided electronically – on the WWW for campus-based students and on diskette for distance students. The first week's lesson is a 25-minute videotaped introduction to the unit. Students receive a handout on how to use a WWW browser to access their resource materials and instructions on how to subscribe to the class discussion list. They are then directed to print a copy of their basic unit materials to ensure that they can use their computer system. Access to IC-Assist support services (see page 101) is provided in case of problems and campus-based students have tutorial support in the laboratory and class (videotape) sessions.

The videotapes have been streamlined for external use and will soon be available on the WWW using streaming video techniques, along with a number of supplementary audio lectures. The resource booklet of newspaper and magazine articles was abandoned for copyright reasons – we could not easily get permission to distribute the materials electronically – and has been replaced by assignment-oriented and more general resource materials written by the author.

To alleviate the workload and improve communications with students, most assignments are now marked by the local tutor; however, the e-mail discussion list remains a major source of information for students. As a consequence, the volume of e-mail and master grade sheet maintenance have become major challenges in the unit's management.

According to the limited feedback available, the students view the support services and assignments positively.

'I liked the detail that went into specifying how much information was needed for each and every section of the report assignment . . . It was easier to prepare because you were certain about how much material had to be handed in for all the different criteria.' (Student evaluation, 1997)

'Good assignment. Overall subject: interesting – one of the better subjects.' (Student evaluation, 1997)

'PS – great course, assignment 2 [group discussion on ethical issue] was a real eye-opener.' (Student e-mail, November 1998)

Many are also enthusiastic about the results achieved in their group discussion or training sessions:

'I hope the attachment has worked as it should have. I have included a copy of the résumé my student produced for his third lesson [training in use of word processor] (he was so proud of it he wanted you to see it) he felt you might want a piece of his work.' (Student e-mail, October, 1998)

IC-Assist

An independent student support service was initiated as a direct result of experiences with this and other units in the revised degree. IC-Assist (previously named the MCHotLine) is staffed with senior students for approximately 35 hours per week during the teaching terms. It provides them with casual employment and is a low cost but high impact face-to-face (on the central campus only), telephone, e-mail, WWW, fax and mail support service. Initially begun as a support for first-year computing students, the service was first expanded to include students studying mathematics and now provides support for students in all of the programmes provided by the faculty, although still with a priority for first-year students.

Many students first meet the IC-Assist staff at basic computer operation sessions during orientation week and soon learn to rely on the service for problems with assignments or computing services, contact with lecturers, and general student support. Other students learn about the service from information brochures or recommendations from their lecturers but soon become even more dependent upon the service. For example, the IC-Assist staff regularly pass messages between students and their tutors or lecturers, investigate the late delivery of resource materials, assist with connecting to a local ISP (Internet Service Provider) and have even been the initial contact for students with allegations of sexual harassment in the computer laboratory.

Class discussion lists

HIC students are encouraged to subscribe to the class e-mail discussion list. Unlike many other class lists operated by the faculty, this list has an open membership, allowing students from previous terms to retain their access and provide input to some of the issues arising on the list. Although the list is unmoderated, the author and most of the unit's campus tutors monitor the list and respond to student queries. Tips posted to the list provide all subscribing students with the same assignment information. As was noted earlier, marks are also posted to the list (student ID number and assignment mark only, no names), allowing students to verify that their assignment marks have been recorded in the class grade sheet.

Many of the messages on the list relate to normal class maintenance issues. Soliciting assistance with assignments is a high priority but students also get involved in discussions of e-mail etiquette, professional ethics, software piracy, plagiarism, etc.

What of the future?

The BInfoTech degree is currently under review at the time of writing (1998) and by the year 2000 or 2001 may become one stream of a multistream degree with the information system and health informatics degrees now also offered by the faculty. While our graduates will still require communication skills, it is possible that there will be major changes in the faculty's approach to teaching these skills to our IT students.

In the meantime, HIC has been successfully delivered to several thousand IT students over six years and seems to have achieved the goal of providing communication skills within the context of the discipline, thus overcoming the alienation experienced with the previous communication unit. The unit has not been formally evaluated in several years, but unsolicited comments from students and a minimum of complaints suggest that it is popular with students. The discipline-oriented assignments, video interviews with practitioners, and extensive electronic study materials receive particular praise. As a student recently commented, 'I think the videos [sic] various perspectives of IT in the community are a realistic approach to learning; it's interesting to see where and how these principles are being applied in real life by real people in real situations.' (Student e-mail, 15 August 1998)

REFERENCES

Lincoln, A (1995) Technonerd terminator, *Information Age*, **1** (3), April, pp 26–33.
Human Issues in Computing web site: http://infocom.cqu.edu.au/85138

12

Mathematics Appreciation

Josefina Alvarez

SUMMARY

Mathematics Appreciation is a terminal course designed for non-science majors, to fulfil their general education requirement in mathematics at New Mexico State University. This case study uses the development of this course as a theme and presents observations on how to motivate mathematically disinclined students by placing mathematics in the context of non-mathematical experiences. Course development has utilized numerous comments from the students. In closing, it is argued that the appreciation of mathematics is in fact a concept to be emphasized in any mathematical course.

The author explains how placing mathematics into its broader environment including its historical and social context, acts to inspire students to learn within a subject which they have previously rejected as too abstract or irrelevant.

INTRODUCTION

Located in Las Cruces, New Mexico, in a mid-size city environment, New Mexico State University-Main Campus (NMSU) is a public (state) institution founded in 1888. About 42 per cent of the NMSU students are Black, Hispanic, or Native American. NMSU satisfies the US Department of Education criteria for minority institution status and the Carnegie Foundation for Education classifies it as a Research University I.

The course Mathematics Appreciation is a single-semester course, mandatory for students not taking calculus. The prerequisites are high school algebra and an adequate score on a Mathematics Placement Examination.

The Department of Mathematical Sciences at NMSU offers each semester 10 to 12 sections with 40 students in each section. The student body is extremely diverse in gender, ethnicity, preparation, attitude towards mathematics, and area of study.

The course is part of the University General Education Program. The characteristics of the programme include use of the library and a literature search, a substantial writing component, a historical context, an international perspective, and a multicultural influence.

The specific goals of this course are to provide students with some understanding of the role of mathematics in civilization and with the ability to read, understand, and use mathematics.

The course does not have a prescribed syllabus. Each instructor is encouraged to pursue her or his own ideas of how to fulfil the goals of the course. Instructors have access to a large collection of classroom materials and guidelines contributed by past instructors and updated each semester. The course has a coordinator who provides guidance to new instructors, updates the materials, and supervises textbook selection for those instructors who choose to use one.

Since the spring of 1994, part of the author's teaching duties each semester has been to teach a section of this course and to serve as course coordinator. What follows is a description of the approach adopted to teach this course.

In the end, what is important is the fundamental role of motivation and illustration in the teaching of mathematics (or any other discipline). This is an underlying concept that transcends any specific course.

WHAT IS MEANT BY MATHEMATICS APPRECIATION?

As HO Pollak (1996) very accurately observed, 'The perception most people have of mathematics has been moulded by their educational experience, and neither the experience, nor its recollection tends to be happy'. Ironically, many people dislike and fear a mislabelled enemy, because they have only seen what David Fowler (1994) calls 'schoolmath', a quite different subject with its own terminology, methods, and beliefs. Although it is true that most non-science majors may have forgotten a good part of their 'schoolmath', the bad feelings about their experience remain.

On the other hand, in spite of the indisputable applicability of mathematics, it is true that it takes some planning to communicate the effectiveness of mathematics to a non-specialized audience.

As a result of all these factors, the dealings of mathematics seem too often closed off as by a high wall. How can this wall be breached, how can mathematics be presented in a way that a passer-by may enjoy it? Better yet, how can a reluctant spectator be lured into becoming, to some extent, a performer? There is no universal recipe for what is required to appreciate mathematics.

However, experience shows that any successful approach should recognize the special characteristics and the wealth of non-scientific knowledge that the students have. In the words of DF Halpern (1997), 'What and how much students learn in any situation depends heavily on their prior knowledge and experience . . . Because students frequently fail to apply what has been taught to them in class to the real world, part of our teaching must be focused on "transferability"'.

It is very effective to present mathematics in several combined ways: as a powerful tool in the students' own business, as a mean to develop effective thinking and communication skills, as a phenomenon of cultural history, and as a collection of fundamental thoughts and ideas.

One of the teacher's tasks is to convincingly present the central role that mathematics has played in people's lives throughout history. Another task is to convey what the physicist Eugene Wigner called 'the unreasonable effectiveness of mathematics'.

This effectiveness was already observed in 1920 by Albert Einstein when he asked 'How can it be that mathematics, being after all a product of human thought independent of experience, is so admirably adapted to the objects of reality?'

HOW TO TEACH MATHEMATICS APPRECIATION

A course on mathematics appreciation should not insist on technical skills. Rather, it should make the best out of whatever skills the students have, typically vague recollection of high school algebra.

This course may be viewed as a mathematics course, where the students are expected to see and do mathematics. In fact, many of the most beautiful and enduring mathematical ideas and their applications have a common sense quality that makes them fairly natural to grasp.

Examples include, the irrationality of $\sqrt{2}$ or that there are infinitely many prime numbers. Or Erathostenes' method to find the circumference of the earth (Figure 12.1).

If Wiles' proof escapes this common sense quality, still the story of Fermat's last theorem is a thriller, nicely staged in the BBC video 'The Proof', which shows that mathematical creativity is as passionate as any other human endeavour. How about counting? One can go a long way using the idea of counting the fingers in one's hand, one, two, three, four, five, or, in other words, establishing a bisection between the five fingers and the collection of five numbers $\{1, 2, 3, 4, 5\}$ (Figure 12.2).

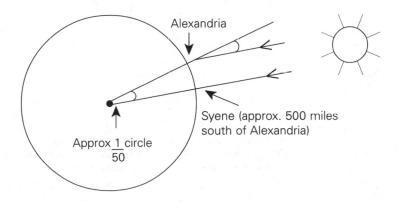

Figure 12.1 *Erathostenes' method to find the circumference of the earth*

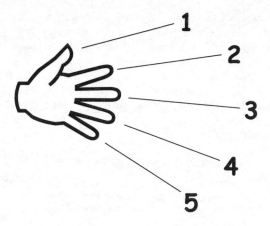

Figure 12.2 *Establishing a bisection between the five fingers and the collection of five numbers*

When collections are allowed to have infinitely many members, some strange things happen. For instance, there are hotels where there is always a vacancy (Figure 12.3). Indeed, imagine a hotel with infinitely many rooms, numbered 1, 2, 3, 4, 5, 6, . . .

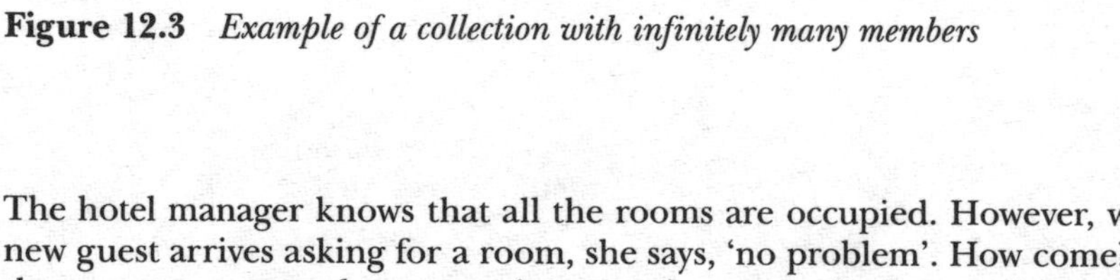

| 1 | 2 | 3 | 4 | 5 | 6 |

Figure 12.3 *Example of a collection with infinitely many members*

The hotel manager knows that all the rooms are occupied. However, when a new guest arrives asking for a room, she says, 'no problem'. How come? Well, the manager moves the person in room 1 to room 2, the one in room 2 to room 3, and so on (Figure 12.4).

Now room 1 is empty.

It is this author's contention that practically every mathematical topic, appropriately organized, can be turned into an engaging presentation.

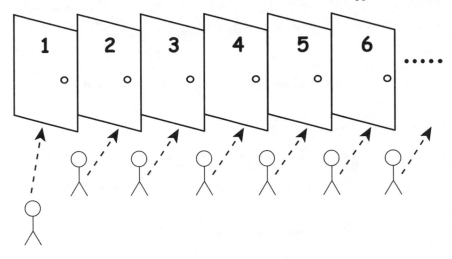

Figure 12.4   *Making room*

The instructional format used is highly interactive, with students doing a significant amount of the work in class, in groups. Students are required to have and use a scientific calculator. The calculator is a good and simple way of fighting the tendency students bring to look for 'the answer', to learn about rounding-up or rounding-down, and to practise little numerical experiments.

Readings from books, journal articles, newspaper and magazine articles are used. In-class activities such as problem solving and discussion, visual materials, and hands-on materials are also included.

One major goal is to exemplify the presence of mathematics outside any 'mathematical environment'. This is what is described to the students as 'accidental mathematics'. For instance, in a newspaper report on an archaeological finding in southern Chile, one can read 'Radiocarbon dating of bone and charcoal . . .' Another article on wine production states that 'Growers prefer small berries, because much of the flavour and colour of grapes is in the skin. Large berries have a lower surface-to-volume ratio, and thus have proportionately less skin'. Yet another article reports on state appropriations for higher education. Apparently, our university has received a positive increase in budget, which, alas, turns out to be negative when corrected for inflation.

Great emphasis is placed on the historical development of concepts, on the recognition of patterns, and on the sociological implications of mathematical information and choices.

Along the semester students are asked to write short opinion essays. They are quite surprised to find subjectivity and the possibility of interpretation in some aspects of a topic frequently thought of as an absolute truth. Besides serving as one of the parameters to measure their learning process, these essays provide me with an informal feedback on their changing views of mathematics.

The following are quotations from their essays:

'Never in any geometry class have I learned who influenced the Greeks!'

'Societies function mathematically as well as is necessary for them.'

'If the human mind has simply manufactured the idea of mathematics, why does it work so well?'

'Mathematics was already there for man to discover and use.'

'The more I write, the more I think mathematics is a "human thing" not an everlasting subject.'

'Mathematics is then as natural for humans as language and communication.'

Students also work on two significant writing assignments based on topics of their choice. As a guide, the students are provided with an extensive list of references.

Lecturing is kept to a minimum. The teacher's role in the classroom is more of a moderator of students' discussions; fortunately the class is located in a classroom with movable furniture that encourages and facilitates cooperative work.

At the start of the semester the students are asked to work on a set of very simple problems that are referred to as 'warm-up exercises'. They are surprised to see that they can actually 'do some math' right from the start and without teacher intervention. These problems prepare the ground from which the branches of the course will grow. For instance, the problem 'An employee's annual salary was increased from $21,582 to $23,103. 'What percentage rate did she get?' uses the same concept of rate that we will use later when we work with populations or investments.

Typically, topics covered include mathematics in ancient civilizations, mathematical ideas of traditional peoples, numbers, modelling population dynamics, consumer mathematics, puzzles and paradoxes, and mathematics in the art of MC Escher.

The teacher proves and discusses some of the formulae to be used. Even very simple formulae, such as compounded interest or annuities, provide powerful examples of mathematics at work. For most students, this is the first time they see how a formula is obtained. It also gives a meaning to algebraic manipulations they may have seen before. Overall, the purpose is to emphasize the continuity and connectedness in the way mathematics develops and progresses. For this purpose, it is crucial to emphasize credible beginnings and links to previous experiences or human needs.

STUDENTS' FEEDBACK

Students are asked to answer the following questionnaires at the beginning and at the end of the course:

Questionnaire 1

I am seeking information on students' perceptions of this course. Your cooperation on filling out this questionnaire will be very useful. One word answers do not give me very much information. Feel free to add any comments. You do not need to write your name on this form. I will ask you to answer another brief questionnaire at the end of the course. I am asking you to write your date of birth to match your answers to both questionnaires. Thank you for your time.

- What does mathematics appreciation mean to you?
- What do you expect to see in this course?

Questionnaire 2

I am seeking information on students' perceptions of this course. Your cooperation on filling out this questionnaire will be very useful. One word answers do not give me very much information. Please, give reasons for your responses, and whenever appropriate give examples. Feel free to add any comments. Your responses will be held in the department's office, and provided to me only after the semester is over and grades are assigned. You do not need to write your name on this form. I am asking you to write your date of birth to match this questionnaire with the questionnaire you answered the first day of class. Thank you for your time.

- How has this class been like or unlike your personal expectations? What parts of the class have been different from what you expected?
- Has your view of mathematics changed? How?
- Which topic was your favourite? Why?
- What topic was your least favourite? Why ?
- Is there anything in this class that you would like to see changed?

Questionnaire 1 is administered at the beginning of the first day of class. This questionnaire helps students reflect on their prior knowledge and attitude towards mathematics. It also gives valuable information on the class profile.

Questionnaire 2 comes after the students have gone through the entire course. It helps them reflect on their learning process and on how this process has changed, or not, their perception of mathematics. It also helps fine tune the course.

In their answers to Questionnaire 1 many students reject the possibility of appreciating mathematics. Their expectations on what they will see in the course are also vague. Many expect to see 'lots of algebra'.

The students' responses to Questionnaire 2 show, for the most part, a very positive change in their attitude towards mathematics. The following quotations illustrate a few responses:

'I expected drudgery of trying to complete copious amounts of stupid problems such as if two pipes fill a pool that is unplugged . . . Instead I worked on things that I can go home and do for myself and my family, like retirement accounts.'

'This class has helped me understand that we need math in everything we do. I did not expect to look at art in a math class. I did not know math could be in art.'

'Math seems more like a philosophy now, a way of perceiving the world instead of something to use only to solve algebraic problems of no pertinent importance.'

'This is the first math class that I have actually enjoyed.'

'I found it refreshing to write essays on mathematical ideas with our opinion rather than just calculating problems.'

The official course evaluation administered by the department also shows a very high level of satisfaction.

CONCLUSION

It could be argued that since this is a terminal course, students gaining an appreciation for mathematics will not have a chance to build on it in future courses. However, it should be observed that mathematicians, and scientists in general, are rarely found among political advisors and policy makers. So, if the educated public opinion has a better understanding of mathematics, this can have a positive influence in their response to the needs of the mathematical community. It can also produce an appreciation for the importance of mathematics in the school curriculum and beyond. Furthermore, individuals' perception of mathematics will undoubtedly influence their children's attitude towards the subject, thus helping to reinforce or break the circle of mathematical avoidance.

In a personal note, to teach mathematics appreciation has had a profound and positive effect in the way this author teaches any other course at the undergraduate or graduate level. Motivation, illustration, and historical development of the concepts are now high priorities when preparing to teach any course.

REFERENCES

Fowler, D (1994) What society means by mathematics, *Focus: Newsletter of the Mathematical Association of America*, April 1994, pp 12–13

Halpern, DF (1997) The war of the worlds: When students' conceptual understanding clashes with their professors, *Chronicle of Higher Education*, **43** (27), 14 March

Pollak, HO (1996) Mathematics: The science of patterns, book review, *Notices of the American Mathematics Society*, November, pp 1353–1354

13

Working with Students to Enhance an Unpopular Course

Anne Arnold and John Truran

SUMMARY

This chapter summarizes work by the authors in listening to non-science students using four different approaches to find out why they were unhappy with a 'service' statistics course, as a first step towards raising their interest.

The authors have different backgrounds – one in statistics, the other in mathematics education. A blend of these skills was particularly valuable in developing a helpful understanding of students' appreciation of the course.

The approaches used were very effective. Journal keeping inspired the students to think more deeply about the course content, and this led to some changes in the course emphasis.

While a small, often vocal, minority remained negative, most found the course to be at least satisfactory, and failures were usually due to non-academic reasons. Finally, finding that the vocal minority was not representative of the class inspired the lecturer to work for still further improvements.

INTRODUCTION

This chapter summarizes the results of a project designed to determine why students reacted unfavourably to a 'service' statistics course, as a preliminary to effecting improvements. The subject concerned is a first-year, compulsory one-semester course in introductory statistics offered mainly for economics, commerce and finance students. The project was supported by two financial grants from the School of Economics.

Students had expressed their dislike of the course through formal university assessments, comments to staff, and indirectly through a high failure rate. Yet to the staff the course seemed practical and relevant, provided relatively small lecture groups, small weekly tutorial groups, and well-advertised consulting times. It was not clear whether the objections were general, or came only from a small group of vocal students.

To identify the problems, Anne Arnold, the lecturer-in-charge, consulted with John Truran, a mathematics educator who had been tutoring in the course while undertaking further studies. We decided that a mixture of statistical and educational skills was likely to succeed in suggesting minor improvements which could be quickly implemented, and major improvements for implementation in later years. This approach proved remarkably effective and revealed a situation quite different from what we had anticipated.

LITERATURE REVIEW

A literature search produced suggestions about teaching methodologies, ways of identifying students' poor understanding and ways of managing courses for more effective teaching, but none of these directly addressed students' dislikes. Gordon (1995) had looked in general at students' affective views of service statistics courses, but we were looking for something more concrete. From our reading, journal keeping seemed to be the most effective first step for our needs.

Journal writing has occasionally been used in mathematics education for assessing the impact of a course on students (Ellerton and Clements, 1996) and seemed to have many potential benefits (Borasi and Rose, 1989). It offered:

- flexibility;

- opportunities for the expression of feelings and opinions;

- potential value for journalists;

- fairly fast feedback;

- weekly contact with students;

- acceptable administrative demands.

JOURNAL PROJECT

So, in first semester, 1997, we tried to gather a stratified random sample of 30 students (about 20 per cent of enrolments) who would keep, for a small monetary incentive, a weekly confidential journal. We endeavoured to select students in a way which would preserve anonymity. Unfortunately, only about 10 of our chosen sample were willing to participate, so eventually we accepted anyone who volunteered. This led to a working list of 17 people, of whom only 13 were fully active.

The group was certainly not representative of the class. About two-thirds were female, compared with one-third in the total enrolment. The journalists tended to be first-language English speakers, and high achievers, who attended tutorials and handed in required work of good standard on a regular basis. There was only one poor student. Hence their responses could only show what able and/or committed students thought of the course, but they were almost all thoughtful and frank.

Erickson (1986: 140) has warned about the importance of obtaining enough and sufficiently varied evidence for substantiating claims, and of being particularly careful to look for disconfirming evidence. We chose our questions carefully to try to obtain this evidence. Other cross-checks came from parallel journals kept by the staff and the three other forms of enquiry described below. The types of issues in the journals included:

- conceptual difficulties identified in published research (eg Cohen *et al*, 1996; Vallecillos Jiménez, 1996) or in previous experience with the course;
- known causes of dissatisfaction;
- higher-order understanding;
- 'housekeeping' issues.

FINDINGS AND CHANGES MADE

Both the lecturer and the journalists found the project to be of great value and the journalists clearly appreciated being encouraged to think through their learning of the topics. The process required us to take all comments seriously, even if we thought 'But we do that anyway,' or 'This student did not bother to listen to what was said'. Altogether, there were five significant successes.

Almost all housekeeping criticisms were accepted and attended to rapidly. This increased students' confidence in our intention to take their comments seriously. That there were few such complaints also boosted the lecturer's confidence. It was reassuring to find that at least some students perceived the subject to be useful, interesting and challenging, and had no major complaints.

This positive feedback encouraged the lecturer to think more deeply about teaching the course, particularly the issue of cognitive learning and levels of understanding. Many students preferred a deterministic, numerical approach with a strong emphasis on rote learning, and in previous semesters much of the course could have been done in this way. However, the journals made it clear that at least some students saw the need for a more flexible, language-based approach to statistical interpretation. Because some of the journal questions required deep understanding and explanation, the students were encouraged to go beyond mechanical answers, to look up notes and to check details in order to clarify and deepen their understanding. They also benefited from being forced to look at both the big picture and the small details every week. So the journalists benefited in several ways and the lecturer gained an insight into what was well taught, what wasn't, and whether there were any misconceptions to be cleared up. It was here that the mix of statistics and education skills proved of most value. As a result, the balance in lectures, tutorials and assessments between doing the calculations and understanding the issues started to change.

The journals also gave us a much better understanding of students' study habits, their motivations and their working constraints. Even though these were good students, they lacked good study skills, and were often constrained by part-time work, illness or family responsibilities. These constraints were more widespread than we had thought and showed that the students were not like the student body of our generation and could not be judged from that point of view (Moore, 1997). Knowing this made it easier to understand their comments and respond to them positively.

Finally, when the complaints were not seen as appropriate, the lecturer's point of view could be explained clearly to all the students. For example, after each lecture handout summaries were given to students, who criticized them as being a very poor textbook. We could explain that they were meant only as a supplement to the textbook, and suggest how to make good use of the different approaches.

CHECKING THE VALIDITY OF THE COMMENTS

We believed that we had understood the opinions of the more committed students. But we still needed ways of listening to the less committed students. Contacting them was not likely to be easy, given the trouble we had had in obtaining journalists.

We decided on three separate approaches. We interviewed students who had re-enrolled in 1998, after previous failure. Then we examined the official course assessment responses from 1997. Finally, we used data from the 1997 course to design an instrument to predict which 1998 students were heading towards failure, and then made contact with these students. Since the 1997 and 1998 cohorts were similar we believed that these three diverse approaches would allow us to assess the general applicability of the journalists' responses. This proved the case.

Interviews with repeating students

Of the 115 students enrolled at the beginning of first semester 1998, about 33 per cent had enrolled previously in the course, some several times. We asked 25 repeating students to attend a structured interview. At the end of the fourth week, nine of the 25 had shown no sign of being involved in the course. Of the remaining 16, 11 had been interviewed. This group was small, but all were happy to be interviewed, seemed honest and open in their replies, and were representative of the 'repeaters'.

When compared with the whole class, there was a higher probability that a repeating student was under 22 years old, was in the economics faculty, and was male. None of those interviewed had difficulties with English and almost all were living at home. About one-third had repeated their final school year, but on the other hand, three had obtained very good grades. All had obtained reasonable tertiary entrance scores. Only two or three expressed a distaste for mathematics. These findings effectively squashed many of the anecdotal reasons for student failure which were often put forward in the tea-room!

But two other features were significant. Many students were working long hours in paid employment, sometimes on night shifts. Many had failed other university subjects as well, in one case nine in two years! Very few of the subjects actually passed had been at higher than a pass grade. These reasons for failure lay outside our control, and were only weakly related to dissatisfaction with the course, or inability to understand it.

This was confirmed by the students, eight of whom had no serious criticism of the course. Two did criticize their tutors, and one expressed criticisms specific to his employment situation. Their criticisms were very similar to those of the journalists, and none blamed the weaknesses they saw in the course for their failure. Students were unanimous in their view that while the course was not terribly exciting, it was a fair course with a reasonable work load. But it was seen as a cumulative subject which was harder to catch up on than more discursive subjects such as economics, so when they tried to cut their losses as examinations approached, they tended to disregard the statistics course. Furthermore, when students did run into difficulties, academic or personal, they did not seek help from others, even though some would have been eligible for extensions or supplementaries on compassionate grounds.

This survey of unsuccessful students certainly gave us more insights into reasons for failure than we had gained from the journalists, but it also strongly confirmed the views of the journalists that the course was a reasonable course which did not deserve the poor reputation it had acquired. But we still needed to see if these views matched those of the silent majority, and of those who enrolled in the course, but whose contact with it was minimal. Since it would be difficult to obtain detailed responses from these groups, we needed to use less personal approaches.

Analysis of SET responses

The university's official Student Evaluation of Teaching (SET) conducted at the end of each course involves students' rating many aspects of the course and the lecturer on a seven-point scale, usually from 'strongly disagree' through 'undecided' to 'strongly agree'. There is some pressure on staff to aim for a mean score of six or more. Yet the results are not representative of the whole class, because attendance at the end of the semester is low. Some questions, such as 'I have understood the concepts presented in the subject' are unlikely to have a constant meaning for all students. Others address issues beyond the experience of most students, such as 'The subject was relevant to the requirements of my profession'. To use the arithmetic mean as an absolute measure of effectiveness for industrial purposes is both unjust and statistically unsound. That it should happen for a statistics course is dishearteningly ironic.

However, we believed that if the SET results were carefully interpreted, they could enable us to hear the voice of the silent majority, and perhaps some minorities as well. A total of 72 SET responses was received, representing 68 per cent of the 106 students who sat the examination or provided a medical excuse.

We first needed to identify the extent to which the answers from each student reflected a single holistic judgement. The first question was 'All things considered, how would you rate this person's effectiveness as a university teacher?' Of the 67 responses, 53 per cent were at levels five or six, and 32 per cent at levels three and four. Only 7 per cent considered the lecturer to be particularly bad, and only 1 per cent extremely good. Almost all responses to subsequent parts covered only levels one–four or four–seven and tended to conform with the initial holistic judgement. A small group responded with a one, six, or seven for almost all characteristics.

We believed that extreme responses from very few students needed to be treated with special caution. For example, 51 per cent of the respondents felt strongly that the lecturer showed concern for students and 39 per cent that she had enthusiasm for teaching. Given that these characteristics are fairly stable in mature adults, the 7 per cent and 6 per cent respectively who felt that she did not show these virtues were most likely to be making judgements based on special or atypical circumstances. On the other hand, if strong views were expressed by a significant minority of students, then they indicated something of importance. For example 20 per cent of 71 respondents felt strongly that the lecturer had failed to stimulate their interest in the subject and 13 per cent felt strongly the other way. Since some of these respondents were not ticking numbers 'down the line', we could see that they were thoughtfully discriminating between competence and ability to stimulate interest, and that their judgements needed to be taken seriously.

So the SET analysis suggested once again that the journalists' responses were essentially correct, but that there was a very small minority of particularly disaffected students who would be difficult to identify because of the confidentiality of SET. In any case, their disaffection would need individual attention, and could not be addressed as a class issue.

Early identification of students 'at risk'

Finally, we needed to examine the views of those who gave early indication of potential failure, many of whom were likely to drop out of the course. We used 1997 data to construct a measure of being 'at risk' based on attendance at the first three tutorials and performance in the first three tutorial exercises and the first formal assignment. Although the predictor was not perfect, it was reasonably good, and easy to calculate, so we decided to use it in week four of 1998.

This identified 51 students as being 'at risk'. All were contacted by letter, warned of their situation, advised about possible courses of action, and asked to discuss the matter with the lecturer. Only nine did so. Of these, four withdrew from the course until a later semester, three had been mis-diagnosed as a result of administrative weaknesses, and only two admitted to any problems. These were given suggestions for improving their study. All of the five who remained in the course passed, one very well. Only one of the nine had any criticism of the course, which confirmed the journalists' judgements yet again.

Such a poor response rate was a surprise. But 25 of the 51 withdrew from the course early enough not to receive a fail grade, and some of these withdrawals may have been as a result of our letter. Whatever the reason, early withdrawal is better than failure. For the first time, too, we were able to see clearly that about half of listed failures were students who had not really engaged with the course in any significant way. This indicated the extent to which the fail rate was exaggerated, and unjustly giving the course a bad name.

CONCLUSION

Given an unpopular subject, our first step in overcoming this was to seek, in a fairly systematic way, students' opinions. The four methods of enquiry provided largely consistent findings. While there were some minor problems in the course which were quickly corrected, the vast majority of students of all levels of ability considered the course to be a reasonable one, probably not very exciting, and difficult to catch up on if work got behind. We identified the size of the small minority who were seriously disaffected, though it was not clear what could be done to overcome their objections. The size of the large minority who never really engaged with the course became more apparent, and some of the reasons for this were identified. Putting the non-engagers aside, the failure rate could not be attributed to serious weaknesses in the course: in many cases it was the result of factors quite outside the control of the university.

But there were much more positive findings still. The methodology we have described here proved to be a useful and cost-effective first step in responding to student dissatisfaction. Our initial question, 'How do we change the course so that students are not so unhappy with it?', was transformed to a much deeper one, 'How do we inspire students and show them how important the course is?' This change of focus has not only provided a much better base for making further improvements but has also led to much improved morale among both staff and students. In particular, at least some students have appreciated and benefited from the opportunities now being provided to respond to the subject in deeper ways than before.

REFERENCES

Borasi, R and Rose, BJ (1989) Journal writing and mathematics instruction, *Educational Studies in Mathematics*, **20**, pp 347–65

Cohen, S *et al* (1996) Identifying impediments to learning probability and statistics from an assessment of instructional software, *Journal of Educational and Behavioral Statistics*, **21** (1), pp 35–54

Ellerton, N and Clements, MA (1996) Researching language factors in mathematics education: The Australian contribution, in *Research in Mathematics Education in Australasia 1992–1995*, eds P Sullivan, K Owens and B Atweh, pp 191–235, Mathematics Education Research Group of Australasia, no place of publication

Erickson, F (1986) Qualitative methods in research on teaching, in *Handbook of Research in Teaching*, 3rd edn, ed MC Wittrock, pp 119–61, Macmillan, New York

Gordon, S (1995) A theoretical approach to understanding learners of statistics, *Journal of Statistics Education*, **3** (3), http://www2.ncsu.edu/pams/stat/info/jse/v3n3/

Moore, DS (1997) New pedagogy and new content: The case of statistics, *International Statistical Review*, **65** (2), pp 123–65

Vallecillos Jiménez, A (1996) *Inferencia Estadística y Enseñanza: un Análisis Didáctico del Contraste de Hipótesis Estadísticas*, Editorial COMARES, Granada, Spain

14

Student-led Investigations to Introduce Statistics

Graham Clarke

SUMMARY

Many students regard the study of statistics with a measure of apprehension and loathing. Nonetheless, along with many other subjects, contemporary biology has a strong quantitative component and the graduate should have at least some understanding and familiarity with a range of statistical methods. This principle also applies in a wide range of other disciplines and the methods described in this chapter can easily be transferred.

To make the relevance of statistics to the students needs more apparent (and therefore more acceptable to them) a course on scientific investigation was developed. While the course included the use of statistics, the focus was directed at how to do science; particularly, but not exclusively, biological science.

The framework around which the learning was developed was a series of student-led investigations from which students obtained data, which they subsequently analysed using statistical packages. The students presented formal reports that detailed the design of their investigations, the results obtained and conclusions reached.

Student feedback indicated that this approach achieved the aim of convincing students that statistics was relevant to their course of study. Furthermore, students felt that by studying the course, which they regarded as fairly interesting, they had developed a reasonable understanding of statistics.

INTRODUCTION

Students who have to study applied statistics as an subject ancillary to their main discipline have very definite negative preconceptions about the topic. The term 'sadistics' for such statistics courses has fairly widespread use. These courses are not in general well received (A'Brook and Weyers, 1996), with many students perceiving them to be a painful and pointless requirement for obtaining their degree (Gal and Ginsburg, 1994).

121

Various factors may act to make these students unreceptive to tuition in applied statistics. Some students didn't enjoy, or were poor at, mathematics at school and their maths anxiety transfers itself to their study of statistics (Gal and Ginsburg, 1994; Gordon, 1997). They may dislike being 'lectured at' in mathematical 'jargon' (Rinaman, 1998) or fail to see the relevance of statistics to the subject they are studying (Buckles, 1995; Gordon, 1997).

Modern biology, however, has a strong quantitative element within it (Gill, 1996) and places great reliance on statistical methodology. Without the application of inferential statistics, experimental reports tend to become descriptive exercises. Clearly then, it is important that the aversion of biology students towards statistics is overcome, at least enough that they obtain an understanding of, and an ability to use, basic statistical methods.

An obvious approach to making statistics more relevant and hopefully more enjoyable to the students is to give the students data from their subject discipline, and ask them to draw inferences from it (Garfield, 1995; Stuart, 1995; Smeeton, 1997). Also, increasingly, statistics courses are being designed which emphasize the principles behind the statistical methods, leaving the 'mathematics' to be done by computer (Bradstreet, 1996; Rinaman, 1998). However, care must be taken to provide the students with sufficient support to enable them to use the computers effectively, otherwise the computers themselves are seen by the students as a barrier to learning (Rinaman, 1998).

In some disciplines, data derived from central or historical sources may be the 'raw material' on which investigators work. However, biological sciences typically require the researcher to take measurements of some organism, and students within the School of Biological Sciences (SBS) have reported that they find biological data stored in computer files 'dry' and 'divorced from reality'. To get around this, and in addition to make it clear to students that good quality measurements and well thought out experimental protocols are a prerequisite of experimental science, a course in experimental methods, introducing elements of philosophy of science, experimental design, statistical analyses and scientific writing was designed for second-year biology students in SBS.

THE COURSE: STATISTICS AND TRANSFERABLE SKILLS

The majority of students in the SBS, University of Wales – Bangor, attend this course in the first semester of their second year. Only a small number of students, taking particular degrees, omit this course, and obtain tuition in statistics elsewhere. The course, run by a biologist who also holds degrees in mathematics and computing, aims to introduce the students to elements of experimental design, statistical analysis and other transferable skills, such as using computers, working in groups, using databases of publications, and scientific writing, as inherent parts of scientific investigation. This is done, in part, by discussing strengths and weaknesses of published research, and also by getting students to undertake small pieces of research of their own choosing.

Students attend lectures on how to carry out observational, survey and experimental investigations, and over the course appropriate statistical methods for analysing results are introduced. These start off with fairly basic descriptive statistics, and move through exploratory data analysis to regression and analysis of variance; various 'non-parametric' methods are included. The use of the statistical techniques are discussed in the context of the aims and objectives of the various pieces of research in a 'light-hearted', 'anecdotal' and as far as possible interactive way, as follows:

'So you see, what we wanted to find out was . . . and so what we did was . . . However, with hindsight this probably wasn't too smart because . . . Can anyone come up with suggestions as to what we should have done?'

These lectures are not delivered from 'on high' and generally turn into 'how to do it' or '20 ways to "cock up" a research project' discussion sessions. They are intended to include practical, relevant and interesting advice on how to get research 'done', while restricting the amount of statistical terminology to that which will facilitate, rather than inhibit, student understanding. Towards the end of each lecture the actual mechanics of using software to carry out the statistical procedures are demonstrated to the class using a computer, running statistical software, linked to an overhead projector.

The lectures are complemented by a series of 'practicals' undertaken by the students, which over the course require increasing statistical and experimental sophistication. During the lectures the type of problem which can be investigated using a particular experimental or statistical methodology is described to the students, and the students are then required to go out and find some question/data which they can investigate using these techniques. The choice of the question is largely left up to the students, though staff are available to discuss with the students whether their ideas are likely to generate the data required. The students can analyse their data using statistics packages running in the school's computer laboratory, where on two afternoons a week academic staff and demonstrators are available to help them with both the use of computers and the use of statistical methods. The students then have to write up a report of their findings for assessment and (copious) feedback. These student investigations frequently find 'another 20 ways to "cock up" a research project', the most common mistakes being a start for discussion in the next lecture.

As the statistical methodology and investigations required of the students become more complex, so the form of the required report is changed. Initially, almost anything handed in is acceptable (to encourage student participation), but as the course progresses, students are encouraged to, then required to write their report in conventional scientific form.

The final piece of coursework is essentially a mini project in which the students have to research a topic, using library and database resources, collect appropriate data, analyse the data properly, and present a tidy, well-structured scientific report. So far this final work has been imaginative and regarded by staff members (SBS, 1997) and external assessors as of a high scientific standard.

Topics investigated by the students include:

- is chocolate an adequate substitute for sex?;
- car parking habits of students;
- effects of water supply on growth of sunflowers;
- how much alcohol is required before male and female students vomit?;
- sand dune stability and plant species diversity;
- correlation between human height and hours slept;
- influence of light and water on cress germination;
- relationship between plant types and invertebrate diversity;
- does one shop sell bendier bananas than another?;
- do birds 'preferentially' deposit droppings on cars of particular colours?

And of course the 'classic' investigation of does the buttered side fall down more often?

While some of these investigations have limited direct relevance to the study of biological statistics, and some of the investigations clearly show flaws in design, analysis or indeed understanding of scientific methodology (or experimental ethics!), these studies do, at the very least, provide plenty of opportunity for formative feedback. Probably more importantly students have the opportunity and 'permission' to 'play' with their developing scientific skills and enjoy themselves as they learn.

OUTCOME

It is undeniably difficult to teach anything to someone not interested in what you are trying to teach! Prior to this new course, a questionnaire survey of SBS students at the end of their second year of study had ranked statistics as 13th in importance out of 14 subjects they had encountered in that year (Buckles, 1995). In contrast, a survey of students who had studied PO1B (Statistics and Transferable Skills Module) revealed that they regarded statistics as very important to the study of biology and the course fairly interesting. Students appreciated the structure and delivery of the course, and while they found it fairly difficult and requiring more time than other courses (often a consequence of learning through doing (Beard and Hartley, 1984; Gnanadesikan *et al*, 1997) they felt that they had acquired at least a basic understanding of statistical methodology (responses to departmental evaluation questionnaire corresponding to median values of 4, 3, 4, 4, 3 respectively on a five-point scale).

While this is only modest praise of the course, given student feedback from statistics courses in previous years, it was still felt by SBS staff to be a noteworthy change in student opinion.

Incidental outcomes include increasing the statistical knowledge of the PhD students who demonstrate on the course and providing a resource for the third-year (and postgraduate) students who 'just happen to drop by' the practical sessions to ask questions about experimental and statistical methods.

Problems

Students initially found the relative freedom to investigate what they wanted off-putting; however, as one aim of this course was to help encourage student autonomy – the ability to chose and solve their own problems – this aspect of the course has been retained, although the reason the students are allowed this choice has been made more explicit to them. While many students managed the course well, several found themselves floundering – particularly with the use of computers – additional drop-in tutorials were arranged so that students having difficulties with any aspect of their assignments could discuss it with members of staff. One unexpected development was that some students spontaneously formed self-help groups to assist each other in working with computers; this beneficial development is now supported and encouraged by allowing students to undertake their research in groups.

CONCLUSION AND EXTENSION

The aim of the course was to encourage students to gain a range of scientific and transferable skills, including, importantly, a basic knowledge of statistics, by showing these skills to be relevant and important in the study of biology (students in SBS have in the past placed much less importance on 'transferable skills' than staff do (Buckles and Clarke, 1997). In this, the course has been a success.

The influence of PO1B on the students' view that statistics is useful to biologists has been enhanced by incorporating the use of statistics into the mainstream teaching of biology in SBS (Chalmers and Fuller, 1996); by encouraging (or requiring) students undertaking practicals in other modules to include statistically-based conclusions in their write up. This helps 'embed', through practice, the statistical knowledge they have acquired in PO1B (Garfield, 1995). Some students have even asked about the possibility of SBS running more advanced statistics courses for them in their third year!

The student learning experience is to be extended by running an additional workshop on 'writing for publication'. Those students who wish to attend will – working in small groups and assisted by members of staff – refine their final assignment report, for incorporation into a book. The hope is that students will then have developed and used skills, from finding a question to address, through collecting data, analysing results and interpreting their findings, to publishing their research; in other words the students will have done 'real' science.

Statistics, from being a not terribly well-regarded ancillary subject, 'Fiction in its most uninteresting form' as Evan Esar (1943) put it, is now seen by SBS students to be a core skill for a researcher in biological sciences.

REFERENCES

A'Brook, R and Weyers, JD (1996) Teaching of statistics to UK undergraduate biology students in 1995, *Journal of Biological Education*, **30**, pp 281–88

Beard, R and Hartley, J (1984) Practical and laboratory teaching, in *Teaching and Learning in Higher Education*, pp 195–214, PCP, London

Bradstreet, TE (1996) Teaching introductory statistical courses so that nonstatisticians experience statistic reasoning, *American Statistician*, **50**, pp 69–98

Buckles, J (1995) An analysis of staff and undergraduate opinion on the value of various teaching approaches, in the School of Biological Sciences, Bangor, BSc thesis, University of Wales, Bangor

Buckles, J and Clarke, GS (1997) A short report on staff and student opinion of the aims of studying biology to degree level and the value of different teaching/learning methods, in *Realising Academic Potential*, vol 2, eds J Fazey and F Poland, pp 5–18, University of Wales, Bangor

Chalmers, D and Fuller, R (1996) *Teaching for Learning at University*, Kogan Page, London

Esar, E (1943) *Esar's Comic Dictionary*, Bantam Doubleday, New York

Gal, I and Ginsburg, L (1994) The role of beliefs and attitudes in learning statistics: Towards an assessment framework, *Journal of Statistics Education*, **2** (2) http://www.stat.ncsu.edu/info/jse/

Garfield, J (1995) How students learn statistics, *International Statistical Review*, **63**, pp 25–34

Gill, P (1996) Can we count on biology?, *Journal of Biological Education*, **30**, pp 159–60

Gnanadesikan M et al (1997) An activity-based statistics course, *Journal of Statistics Education*, **5** (2) http://www.stat.ncsu.edu/info/jse/

Gordon, S (1997) Students' orientation to learning statistics, in *People in Mathematics Education*, eds F Biddulph and K Carr, pp 192–99, proceedings of the 12th Annual Conference of the Mathematics Education Research Group of Australasia Inc, University of Waikato

Rinaman, WC (1998) Revising a basic statistics course, *Journal of Statistics Education*, **6** (2), http://www.stat.ncsu.edu/info/jse/

SBS (1997) *TQA Self Assessment Document*, School of Biological Sciences, University of Wales, Bangor

Smeeton, N (1997) Statistics education in medicine and dentistry, *The Statistician*, 47, pp 521–27

Stuart, M (1995) Changing the teaching of statistics, *The Statistician*, **44**, pp 45–54

15

Work-based Assessments to Improve Learning

John Flynn

SUMMARY

Mature students who are line managers in the local public or private sector and who are studying for a three-year, part-time Masters in Business Administration (MBA) provide the setting for the example provided in this chapter.

Poor appreciation of quantitative methods has implications for the workplace and managerial decision making. Many with numeracy and literacy limitations do not see it as a problem, carrying the attitude to the workplace and thus causing employers dissatisfaction.

In the example utilized here, the practical application directly promotes the usefulness of quantitative methods by introducing software to support decision making. This occurs first of all in the classroom but is assessed with reference to work conducted in the student's office or factory.

Work-based assessment enhances the taught aspect by developing a critical evaluation of, and competency in, the numerical techniques. Students are sufficiently inspired to advance the techniques into their work environment, through the self-collection of data and selection of appropriate analysis and software.

INTRODUCTION

Part-time MBA students who purchase an education, possibly without sponsorship, have clear objectives to become more proficient in people skills, organizational skills, management thinking, etc. Our quantitative methods teaching is supported from one specialist textbook rather than management books, as they tend to relegate quantitative methods to the back end.

Quantitative methods textbooks can be very prescriptive in manner, overflowing with technically good work but racing ahead in terms of language and, importantly, guidance for the student towards workplace application. After an introductory chapter, students have to eat from a fast service of management science, statistics or operations research.

The importance of quantitative methods on American MBA programmes has, in the past, been undermined because nearly 40 per cent of personnel teaching the required 'statistics' sequence regarded statistics as a secondary activity (Rose, Machak and Spivey, 1988), a disturbing conclusion. We wonder if this is the case in the United Kingdom, because it would not happen in the teaching of accounting, marketing, finance, personnel management, and so on.

Our approach to overcoming student disinterest is to create, in class contact time, a mixture of formal teaching and computer work. Appropriate theory and examples are analysed with a software teaching package (Management Scientist, 1998) to deliver calculations and achieve quick progress in getting to the answers. Assignments are vital, not only in terms of assessment, but for the motivation to model a problem, obtain results and evaluate the solutions. Students are encouraged to discuss the models they have used, even to the extent of rejecting them.

The institution

The University of Lincolnshire and Humberside is one of the United Kingdom's newer vocational universities, based on three sites at Kingston-upon-Hull, Lincoln and Grimsby. The university is a prominent member of the Association of Commonwealth Universities, with strategic strength in its regional and international partnerships. Over many years, there has been support from British Petroleum in the development of innovative teaching and learning strategies.

Some 13,000 students attend courses on-campus, and the university travels to several thousand off-campus students through a worldwide distribution of partner institutions.

The Hull Business School, the largest school in the university, has about 3,000 full and part-time undergraduate and postgraduate students taught on-campus, and another 2,000 students take its degrees around the world.

Teaching the part-time MBA

The part-time MBA is contained within the Hull Business School, being serviced by tutors with appropriate industrial experience and academic backgrounds. Assessment strategies were designed to develop the students' critical and independent thinking processes.

The part-time, day-release mode of study enables five units a week to be addressed, with the following objectives:

- provide the appropriate knowledge and skills to manage effectively up to senior management level;

- develop the capacity of students to manage their own learning and development;

- develop the power of critical enquiry, logical thought, creative imagination and independent judgement in a context of application.

The quantitative methods unit is firmly established in the first year of the MBA programme (Certificate in Management Studies) which covers:

- managing self and others (including the team, conflict and change);
- management resources and functions (human resource management, business environment, operations and marketing);
- management information (quantitative methods and information technology);
- financial accounting and financial management.

The quantitative methods unit is, in fact, titled Business Analysis and Decision-Making. Its 22.5 hours of contact time over 15 weeks takes the majority share of the management information module.

The nature and numbers of students

Students are, generally, locally based in full-time positions of management or supervision in East Yorkshire or North Lincolnshire. Few, if any, are overseas students. In the Hull district, the manufacturing sector is strong and the service sector supports a city of 250,000. Sadly, from the Hull district there is less uptake of higher education, about one in 10, than the UK national average, about one in three (Knowles, 1998). Only one in seven from the Hull district has gained two or more A levels at school or college (A level is the national qualification that is attained at the typical exit point from secondary education, aged about 18 or 19 years).

Annually, the MBA recruits about 45 students into three cohorts. Students are typically aged from 25 to 45 years, and may, of course, be 10 to 30 years on from their last formal mathematics education at school!

Some who enter this part-time postgraduate programme may be without a first degree, but are allowed onto the programme due to their experience and commitment. It has been known for a student to have no school qualifications, but have 1,000 people reporting to him or her at a local company!

QUANTITATIVE METHODS IN THE CURRICULUM

The quantitative methods unit partners the managerial theories and games and academic focus on finance, marketing, human resource management, etc.

An undergraduate business degree would cover a large proportion of the following quantitative methods material: descriptive statistics, probability concepts and distributions, hypothesis tests, regression, sampling, graphical work, time series analysis.

By the time a student encounters our quantitative methods unit the syllabus covers the following, at a level and pace commensurate with a postgraduate course: probability, normal distribution, forecasting and time series, linear programming, critical path analysis (project management).

Somewhat dangerously, we assume that the undergraduate areas are 'understood' so as to move on quickly. We then wonder whether the undergraduate areas are learned while studying our unit so as to complete the ideal education.

There can be important psychological effects as a result of being non-numerate and lacking in confidence, creating anxiety suffered by students with mathematical worries. This is exemplified by the student bias against production and operations management type courses in the United States (Desai and Inman, 1994).

We could also debate whether quantitative methods are badly taught – or badly learned. Perhaps quantitative methods tutors are too non-specialist, or too academic – or too good!

MOTIVATION AND INTEREST

There has been wide debate about the role of quantitative methods at university level. It has been argued that syllabuses have been set by tradition and should undergo a process of radical redesign to resolve the problem of 'user-friendliness' (Wood, 1994), so that people learn what is actually useful to them in the context in which they will use quantitative methods.

Another view was that students must be given an intuitive and relevant base rather than the traditional statistical grounding (Fridjhon, 1994).

Barman, Buckley and DeVaughn (1997) discussed the education problems of Management Science, saying 'Obtaining the solution to a problem receives the majority of attention. Other important steps such as assumptions, data collection, validation and implementation receive insufficient attention. Most business problems warrant a sound qualitative analysis, and the quality of the solution depends upon the extent to which such issues are considered'.

The course team has found that the students themselves answer the question of motivation as they begin to recognize that it is not a mathematics course. There is decision making which can be securely analysed with what is taught in the quantitative methods unit, and the solution is in their hands with timely analysis.

Description of approach adopted

Our curriculum for quantitative methods is a blend of statistics and management science, and we heartily endorse current textbook promotion of the spreadsheet, or an accompanying teaching package, to facilitate curriculum coverage.

Our MBA students have to produce two individual assignments, each of 1,500 words, and take a 45-minute multiple-choice test. We have, with some compassion, thought hard about how to help students to achieve the assessment.

There is some guidance on the way that the best working relationship with students might develop (Greenan, Humphreys and McIlven, 1997). They quote Peter Davis (1995) of the Institute of Management who said that employers are now demanding a number of qualities when recruiting new staff. These include the ability to communicate effectively, the ability to work with others, functional numeracy and familiarity with IT. These core skills should become an integral part of all education and training programmes at all levels.

For several years we have worked on the two ideas of functional numeracy and familiarity with IT. We have retained some of the heavy theoretical mathematical theory but permitted student opportunities for input and digression when formal lecturing is occurring. We work through the process rather than the content of the analysis. 'Ten commandment' type rule sets are less dogmatically promoted than if we were interested in rigorous mathematical theory.

We aim to achieve a practical level of quantitative methods rather than a theoretical base of techniques. The tutor is an 'encourager', a coach rather than a distant educator who delivers the mathematical techniques from a blackboard. The emphasis is on personal adoption of data, reflection about the work-based motives, and a dependence on the management scientist software to achieve the answers and enable some progress on problem solving.

We have adopted one textbook (Anderson, Sweeney and Williams, 1998). It is packed with a variety of good case studies, and offers graded opportunities for practice and re-enforcement work.

In the decision-making process, we have to concede that intuition has to take over at some point from the mathematical analysis. Quantitative methods should only be seen as an aid to the most efficient decision making. Subjective knowledge and analysis always complement or even override the numerical analysis, but this is dangerous as it contradicts the principle of objective (unbiased) analysis.

PRACTICAL WORK

Our accompanying teaching package, the Management Scientist, gets students working very quickly on data entry, checking, calculations and analysis, with progression to discussion of the results. This is an important achievement for students, and we then urge reflection on the results rather than seeing the calculations as being the endpoint.

For example, students are quickly weaned off the graphical solution to a linear programming problem because it is a limited approach. The software assists the 'what-if' (follow-up) analysis in which students change the parameters in the problem. Case studies in market research, petrol blending, financial analysis or production scheduling offer a variety of stimulating scenarios in which students have fun through making more money by increasing the resources.

By using the software managerially, with common sense and in small groups, students become interested in the answers to problems. This is seen as important as deriving the algebraic formulae for the problem in an academic fashion. We recognize that 'getting the hands dirty' within 30 minutes of meeting the technique will produce confidence in using quantitative methods for a business purpose. We have seen this to be true for two other aspects of our curriculum, namely forecasting and critical path analysis (project management).

In the computer laboratories, after being taught that there are forecasting techniques, students quickly obtain the results of fitting four time-series models, ie exponential smoothing, moving average, linear regression and seasonal models, by the use of software. We then discuss the best fitting model, as it might have significant weaknesses, eg it may only forecast one period ahead, or there may be an assumption in the model that inhibits its rightful use in a company.

In teaching critical path analysis, students realize that the final requirement is usually project monitoring and control, so as to compare performance achievement with planned activity levels. It is not enough, we say, to have a project plan and spend hours drawing networks and compiling analyses by hand. Students at the business level want to know about corrective action, modification to working forecasts and redevelopment of corporate goals. We teach this in the laboratory, with immediate access to Microsoft Project, so as to get students involved with planning a project on the computer.

WORK-BASED ASSESSMENT

We emphasize critical analysis of the methods as a central part of our teaching and assessment. The objective is to give disinterested students confidence in application of quantitative methods for the longer-term corporate benefit.

The assignment question would incorporate a typical open-ended piece, such as described above, and we would want students to synthesize the numeracy with the theory. We offer the chance to discuss a statement such as: 'Present aspects of forecasting techniques which should, as a minimum, include the following deliverables for the scenario of a graph, assumptions, forecasts and other managerial requirements'. Subsequently, students have to: 'Discuss the management issues which are addressed in using forecasting techniques in your workplace'.

One year we found that a whole class gathered data from their firms. Some had spent a long time finding it, but it was their own data! Analyses are more fruitful as students establish ownership (the Royal Statistical Society strongly advised this at their annual conference in 1995). Work-based assignments are a powerful incentive, because the marking scheme focuses on assumptions and limitations, with emphasis on critical thought, checking of assumptions, 'what-if' analysis, weaknesses of models, and so on.

Students are responsible for delivering a judgement on the best answer, eg which forecast method to trust, or which resource to increase next on a pound-for-pound basis. Working towards the case study answers in the textbook creates confidence. We then ask for their personal, professional interpretation in their workplace.

Assignment marking scheme

For a quantitative methods assignment, generally a case-study, our eight-point marking scheme emphasizes the direction required (distribution of percentage marks in parentheses) for the student to develop, perhaps prescriptively, a management report which:

- assesses the quality and appropriateness of the data (10 per cent);

- demonstrates understanding of analytical approaches available (10 per cent);

- judges the most appropriate analytical approach (10 per cent);

- covers the numerical data analysis (15 per cent);

- comments on the implication of the analysis within the scenario (10 per cent);

- discusses the assumptions and limitations of the analysis (10 per cent);

- provides evidence of further reading and work outside the classroom sessions (20 per cent);

- is presented and communicates clearly, with referencing in an academic fashion (15 per cent).

The requirement for accurate data handling is not relaxed, but the student must exert responsibility for the company in terms of evaluation and referenced work.

EVALUATION

Routine analysis on annual cohorts of students focuses on their careers, their pre-unit impression of quantitative methods as a subject, and their post-unit views about the assignments, the textbook and the computer package.

Students appreciate the unit as concrete. Management issues get aired, calculations get 'rubbished' (especially the normal distribution tables!) and our laboratory work is at the mercy of our computer network.

However, in-depth, formal evaluation by questionnaire of the quantitative methods unit normally confirms that things go well on the aspects that are under our control. It is clear that the impact of an assignment increases the average student satisfaction score in comparison with portions of the syllabus which are not assessed, mainly through the personal input from the student in the work-based reflection.

Examiners' comments

An external examiner was quite positive, and slightly amazed, that linear programming could be taken up so well by students. We put this down to the strength of the practical aspects of the unit. At other times, rapid feedback from the first assignment was noted as helping students to evaluate their performance on the core skills mentioned earlier, an area often of some anxiety.

CONCLUSION

There is place within an MBA course to draw on the people side of a manager's portfolio of abilities and talents in a quantitative methods unit. Decision making is associated with a combination of scientific, factual evidence and human values and students appreciate the practical side of this analysis.

We acknowledge that textbook quantitative methods do not easily get transferred to a complex business problem, but students can make a confident approach on the basis of the quality of the assignments when they address their workplace requirements. Their investigations include model limitations, analysis, feedback, etc within the context of their company. It may even open the way to a recruitment question: 'What sort of person do we need to employ in order to produce good management science work for the benefit of the company?'

Students approve of a practical approach, from which we agree with the teaching motto of 'Tell me and I forget, show me and I remember, involve me and I understand'. Judgement and experience are complementary attributes to the facts and data when analysing a problem. Studying the assumptions and limitations, comparison and evaluation are important aspects of a quantitative methods unit. Work-based assignments are more appropriate than prescriptive assignments where the calculations are the objective.

Strategy, needs, resources, technology and its availability, and closer collaboration with the local industry are all factors of some relevance to the future development of appropriate training in quantitative methods.

REFERENCES

Anderson, D, Sweeney, D and Williams, T (1998) *Quantitative Methods for Business*, 7th edn, South-Western College Publishing, Cincinnati

Barman, S, Buckley, MR and DeVaughn, WLA (1997) Pedagogical concerns in business education, *Society for the Advancement of Management Journal*, **62**, pp 28–35

Davis, P (1995) A Skilled Workforce is the Target, *Management Today*, September, p 5

Desai, K and Inman, R (1994) Student bias against POM (production and operations management) coursework and manufacturing, *International Journal of Operations and Production Management*, **14**, pp 70–87

Fridjhon, P (1994) Fourth International Conference on Teaching Statistics (ICOTS 4), vol 2

Greenan, K, Humphreys, P and McIlven, P (1997) Developing work-based transferable skills for mature students, *Journal of Further and Higher Education*, **21**, pp 193–204

Knowles, J (1998) Aiming high: The Access to Higher Education Project, *The Regional Review*, **8**, pp 19–21

Management Scientist Version 4.0 for Windows (1998), South-Western College Publishing, Cincinnati

Rose, EL, Machak, JA and Spivey, WA (1988) A survey of the teaching of statistics in MBA programs, *Journal of Business and Economic Statistics*, 6, pp 273–82

Wood, M (1994), Towards a rational statistics curriculum for managers and other professionals, Fourth International Conference on Teaching Statistics (ICOTS 4), vol 2

16

The Biology of Numbers

Philip Hammond, Jim Aiton, Gareth Hughes and Ian Nimmo

SUMMARY

It is a paradox that, while the subject becomes increasingly quantitative, many students still elect to study biology in the hope that they will avoid the numerical challenges they had previously associated with chemistry and physics at school. When biology students arrive at university, they may not like or even understand the need for mathematics, but by graduation it is essential that they have become numerate scientists.

This chapter describes the introduction of two very similar courses into two Scottish universities. Each course is designed to teach and reinforce the understanding and use of basic quantitative skills in a biological context.

The courses aim to give the students confidence while taking account of the diversity of their mathematical backgrounds. Teaching these skills early on emphasizes the importance of quantitative rigour and alleviates the need for later duplication or repetition of teaching effort.

By using specific examples from the biological sciences, the authors aim to make students aware of the importance of quantitative skills to solve biological problems. While it would be optimistic to conclude that all students are happy converts to quantitative biology, the shift away from a lecture-based course to a much more self-directed course has been popular with the students and shows evidence of leading to better qualified graduates in the future.

INTRODUCTION

Members of staff involved in teaching core mathematical skills in biological sciences departments at the Universities of Edinburgh and St Andrews have collaborated in the development of their courses, designed to improve the mathematical skills of biology students. The Quantitative Biology (QB) course at Edinburgh began in 1991/92, when a new first-year curriculum in biological sciences was introduced. The previous Quantitative Biology course had covered mathematics, statistics and physics, but under the new curriculum, each of these disciplines was given its own 'half course'. The Quantitative Methods in

Biology (QMB) course at St Andrews was introduced in 1996/97 and was based partly on Edinburgh's QB course and the experiences of those involved in running it during the preceding five years. Both courses aim to provide first-year students with mathematical and related quantitative skills, essential for their degree courses in the biological sciences. The two courses also aim to refresh and reinforce students' confidence in their abilities to handle numerical data.

The overall aim is to introduce, and reinforce, basic quantitative skills within a biological context. We want all students to achieve a certain standard in the knowledge, understanding and application of quantitative methods, so that subsequent studies can concentrate on their chosen discipline within biological sciences. Successful teaching of core mathematical skills at the beginning of students' university careers not only emphasizes the importance of quantitative rigour but also alleviates the need for duplication or repetition of teaching effort during subsequent years.

Students entering the University of Edinburgh or the University of St Andrews to study for the Scottish four-year honours degree in one of the biological sciences are admitted to the Faculty of Science and Engineering or Faculty of Science, respectively, and often have very diverse educational backgrounds. Some may not have studied biology prior to admission to university and these prospective biologists bring a very wide range of qualifications in mathematics.

This diversity of mathematical competencies in new students is a serious concern to those of us involved in teaching in the biological sciences. Current trends in biology require ever more quantitative approaches to the understanding of concepts and to the analysis of scientific data, in contrast to what was historically a more descriptive approach to the subject. It is a paradox of modern biology that, while the subject is becoming more and more quantitative, many students still elect to study biology in the hope that they will avoid the numerical challenges they had previously associated with chemistry and physics at school.

When biology students arrive at university, they may not like or even understand the need for mathematics; but by graduation it is essential that they have become numerate, biological scientists. Our students must pass the QB or the QMB modules in order to proceed to the honours biology degree courses. At Edinburgh, the first-year intake in biological sciences is approximately 450 students. All those who lack mathematical qualifications beyond the English GCSE or Scottish Standard Grade (examinations taken at age 15 or 16), or a grade C in Scottish Higher (the examination used as qualification for entry to university), read the QB course as one of six modules. Most of those who are better qualified read a physics course, which occupies the same timetable slot; statistics is part of the second-year curriculum. Typically, the QB class thus comprises students without substantial previous mathematical qualifications, either because they have not previously studied mathematics, or because they have tried and been unsuccessful. At St Andrews, QMB is a mandatory five-credit module for all first-year students (approximate intake 150), except for those taking a mathematics module, taken in addition to six other 15-credit modules. The better-qualified students have a chance to take and pass the assessment before the course begins.

COURSE DESIGN

When the Edinburgh QB course began in 1991/92, it consisted of lectures covering the mathematical material in the syllabus, together with tutorials, laboratory work (allowing students to collect their own data) and computer laboratory sessions (allowing students to describe, analyse and summarize the data they had collected). Although the course was successful to the extent that a large majority of students reading the course completed it to the satisfaction of the examiners (first-year courses at the University of Edinburgh are externally examined), the contribution of the lectures to this success was debatable. The lectures were, in general, both poorly attended during the course and poorly rated by students in subsequent course feedback questionnaires. It is easy to see why this should be the case. First, lectures in mathematics are, perhaps inevitably, perceived as rather theoretical in content by students of biological sciences, the majority of whom are more interested in experimentation. Second, lectures proceed at a pace dictated by the lecturer. Even experienced lecturers found the optimum pace difficult to judge, given the wide range of numerical aptitude within the class. For those to whom mathematics came easily, this pace was often too slow, and they switched off because they were bored. Others switched off because the pace was too fast for them, or panicked at the first sign of an equation on the blackboard. Third, and perhaps most importantly, mathematics is a discipline which, more than any other, can best be understood by doing rather than listening.

In order to encourage students to acquire basic quantitative skills, it is essential for them to become much more active participants in the learning process. In an attempt to achieve this engagement in the development of practical mathematical skills, the Edinburgh QB course abandoned mathematics lectures in 1995/96 and has since been based instead on the use of a self-teaching workbook, supported by tutorials. This approach was adopted by the St Andrews QMB course from its inception in 1996/97.

Course aims

At the outset of both courses, the importance of mathematics to biology is clearly enunciated to the students; otherwise many fail to appreciate the importance or relevance of quantitative methods. The overall aim is to get each student to a certain standard in understanding and using quantitative methods in biology, enabling them to appreciate the parts of the biology curriculum they will meet in second, third and fourth years that require applications of these methods. The QB and QMB courses are designed neither to push students to their intellectual limits nor to turn them into mathematicians.

The specific aims include:

- to *appreciate the importance* of a basic knowledge of quantitative methods in the context of understanding biology. Students should finish the course knowing why basic mathematics and statistics are useful in biology;

- to *overcome any 'equation-phobia'*. For students who find mathematics difficult, the aim is at least to get them to the stage where they don't panic about it;

- to *learn the basic quantitative skills* essential to obtaining an honours degree in biological sciences. The courses cover the basics; they are not intended to be all encompassing. They should provide a reference when, in future, ideas are encountered which assume this basic knowledge;

- to *gain some transferable skills* in quantitative approaches. Quantitative skills are highly transferable to a wide range of vocations beyond biology.

The workbook

The workbook is a self-teaching book, which allows students to work through the material in the course in their own time and, within limits, at their own pace. Students may work on their own or in small, self-assembled groups. In Edinburgh, the timetable slots previously used for lectures (two per week) have been retained and are designated 'QB workbook time' to give some indication of the length of time that we think is the minimum that should be devoted to the workbook on a weekly basis. In St Andrews, students study the workbook in their own time. Key areas were identified as being essential for biology students to master as the core of their mathematical skills. These include: manipulation and solution of simple equations; construction and use of graphical representations of linear and non-linear relationships; understanding and use of exponents and logarithms; understanding rates of change and the concept and purpose of differentiation.

The workbook covers these areas in chapters, which introduce particular topics. These include: numbers, algebra and straight lines; exponential growth and indices; representing and measuring change; logarithms; and curved line relationships. Each chapter contains lots of examples, most of them biologically motivated, and exercises, with the answers given at the end. Appendix 16.1 (page 145) shows a workbook example of using proportional relationships to calculate concentrations. Appendix 16.2 (page 146) shows part of another example of a graphical analysis of the effect of an insecticide on the fruit fly, in which students use a logarithmic transformation of the data.

When the course is over, students keep the workbook for future reference. They can refer back to it during their university careers and even beyond.

The most important advantage of teaching through the workbook is that a step-by-step approach to explanation can be adopted. Students encountering material that is new or 'difficult' can adjust their pace as appropriate in those sections, and speed up when they meet more familiar material. As a general rule, the approach adopted in the presentation of material in the workbook is to look at specific examples and then generalize from them. The mathematicians' approach tends to be the reverse, a process that many biology students find more difficult to follow. Textbooks aimed at explaining mathematical concepts to biologists tend to go too fast, too quickly. A welcome exception to this is a book aimed specifically at the biology student uneasy with calculations and equations (Burton, 1998). A workbook is also cheap to produce and can be tailored to meet the changing needs of biology students and of other courses in the biology curriculum.

Tutorials

The workbook is designed to be used in conjunction with weekly tutorials. Each chapter culminates in a sheet of questions on the material covered, and each week the students are required to hand in their answer sheet in advance of the tutorial. The tutorials are intended as a forum for the students to go over the previous week's block of work, to raise and discuss any points that are giving them difficulty and to try further examples of problems related to the current topic. Tutors get advance warning of difficulties that have been encountered from the answer sheets handed in by the group.

An additional aim of tutorials is that the students benefit from working in a group, with those who do understand a particular topic helping those who are having difficulties in following that aspect of the course. The success of this depends very much on the dynamics of a particular tutorial group, of course; but the point is that instilling the self-teaching ethic seems to encourage self-help between students. Once the lecture has been removed as the principal source of information, students seem more willing to try a range of alternatives.

Tutors should understand the students' difficulties and be able to help them. We have found that fellow biologists, rather than mathematicians, are best suited to this role. Our experience is that many mathematicians do not appreciate how basic are the difficulties faced by many biology students and are thus unable to provide assistance at the appropriate level. In St Andrews, second-year postgraduate students act as tutors and include this as part of their formal postgraduate training. This has the advantages of giving them revision of the mathematics they covered (or did not cover) as undergraduates, and giving them experience of running a structured tutorial as a stepping stone between demonstrating practicals and running a full, open-ended tutorial. To the students, postgraduates as tutors may not be so daunting as lecturing staff. And the staff time invested in training postgraduates as tutors is more than saved by teaching staff not running tutorials.

ASSESSMENT

A point of difference between the two courses is in the methods of assessment. In Edinburgh, the QB course is assessed by means of a practical report, a two and a half hour class examination, and tutorial performance. Students whose performance in all these elements is satisfactory are granted an exemption from the degree examination in the course. The course runs during the first 'half year' (October–January), after which the exemptions are granted. The degree examination is in June (with a re-sit opportunity in September), so, for those who must sit the examination, the workbook represents a useful source for revision. The degree and class examinations are identical in format. Both comprise six questions, from which the students may choose four. Some of the questions pose mathematical problems in an explicitly biological context, others are solely mathematical. Students are allowed to bring their workbook to the examinations, along with other course material and a calculator of their choice. The 'open book' format to examination is to simulate 'real life' in which students will have access to resources. It also means that the test is one of doing rather than simply remembering. The examination questions are designed to occupy 30 minutes, but we have found that an extra 30 minutes is required if students are to take proper advantage of the 'open book' format of the examinations. The available data suggest that overall pass rates and, in particular, the rate at which exemptions are awarded, have increased since the workbook was introduced (Davie *et al*, 1997; Table 16.1).

Table 16.1   *Assessment statistics for the Edinburgh QB course, data are number of students (percentage of enrolments in parentheses)*

Year	Enrolment	Exempted (January)	Passed (June)	Passed (September)	Passed (Overall)
1997/98*	157	120 (76)	26 (17)	4 (3)	150 (96)
1996/97*	150	99 (66)	34 (23)	14 (9)	147 (98)
1995/96*	133	86 (65)	34 (26)	6 (5)	126 (95)
1994/95	143	68 (48)	54 (38)	8 (6)	130 (91)
1993/94	183	115 (63)	45 (25)	2 (1)	162 (89)
1992/93	190	100 (53)	50 (26)	22 (12)	172 (91)
1991/92	130	69 (53)	51 (39)	5 (4)	125 (96)

* workbook years

In St Andrews, the QMB course is assessed using objective testing. This is achieved in a paper-based multiple-choice question (MCQ) examination, which is subsequently marked by an optical mark recognition system. The benefits of this are two-fold. First, automated objective testing lends itself to the quick turn-around of assessments, so students are able to receive rapid feedback on their performance. Second, objective testing provides a wealth of information on student performance and is particularly useful for establishing mastery criteria that must be met in order for a student to obtain a pass. Areas of strength and weakness for individuals, and the class, can be readily identified and this aids the evolution and improvement of the course. Banks of MCQs have been created to examine the main areas of mathematical knowledge in which we expected the students to show competency.

The difference in assessment methods reflects the fact that the Edinburgh QB course has evolved from a lecture-based to a workbook-based course, whereas the St Andrews QMB course used the workbook approach from its inception. The important point here is that, when developing a course to teach mathematics to biology students, the method of assessment must be considered as an integral component of the course design. This may require investment of resources. In St Andrews, financial support was received as part of a Scottish Higher Education Funding Council teaching initiative awarded to the university.

In St Andrews, students have the option of taking a pre-test before the course begins and, if successful, they are awarded the five-credit pass in the module and need not participate further in the course. This means that tutorial resources can be concentrated on those in most need. In practice, however, relatively few students elect to take this pre-test since they are often aware of their mathematical limitations. Having completed the six tutorials, students can take the test, and should they fail, they can retake the examination within a two-week period. In some selected cases a period of intensive tutoring may be required to help students overcome serious misconceptions and/or a lack of understanding.

COURSE EVALUATION

In Edinburgh, the first-year curriculum is administered by the Biology Teaching Organization (BTO). This includes the coordination of course evaluation (to prevent 'questionnaire fatigue' on the part of students asked to evaluate every course, every year). Typically, QB is assessed by means of a formal BTO questionnaire in alternate years. In the years between questionnaires, informal course evaluation is carried out in tutorial groups at the end of the course. Students may raise problems they encounter during the course either informally, with their tutor, or more formally, through the BTO-administered first-year staff–student liaison committee. Comments made by students are one of the stimuli, along with comments made by tutors and by other members of staff that lead to changes in the workbook from year to year.

Table 16.2 shows questionnaire responses for the two years immediately before, and the two immediately after, the introduction of the workbook, suggesting that gains have been made in clarity of explanation since the introduction of the workbook (Davie *et al*, 1997). Since the introduction of the workbook, the QB course has also been formally evaluated as part of the Quality Assessment in Cellular and Molecular Biology at the University of Edinburgh in 1997. The report found that 'the Quantitative Biology course dealt admirably with students with diverse abilities in mathematics' (http://www.shefc.ac.uk:80/shefc/publicat/qapubs/biolcell/EDINBURG.HTM).

Each chapter of the St Andrews workbook ends with a 'reflective diary' page on which students are encouraged to record their thoughts in real time as they work though the workbook and hand in at the end of the course. Questions include:

- What did you think was good about the workbook in this chapter?

- What did you not like about it?

- How do you think it could be improved?

- Were the tutorials useful for understanding the material in this chapter?

Response has been variable but has helped to improve the workbook.

Table 16.2   *Questionnaire responses relating to the evaluation of lecture/workbook presentation for the Edinburgh QB course; data are numbers of student responses on the five-point scale indicated*

	Was the material in the *workbook* explained clearly?						
	Very clear	1	2	3	4	5	Very hard to follow
1996/97		5	30	19	12	3	
1995/96		2	24	24	26	4	

	Was the material in the *lectures* explained clearly?						
	Very clear	1	2	3	4	5	Very hard to follow
1994/95		2	4	7	21	25	
1993/94		26	12	21	28	26	

WIDER APPLICABILITY

Although first-year biology students tend to be less quantitatively inclined than those in the other sciences, the approach described here is also suitable for chemistry and physics. In St Andrews, a course based on that described is being used in the School of Chemistry to ensure that all students have reached the minimum standard of mathematics required to study this subject at honours degree level. Geophysicists at Edinburgh have shown an interest in the QB workbook and asked if they could evaluate it as a way of allowing their students to acquire basic mathematical skills, where necessary.

The workbook approach need not be limited to the teaching of mathematics. Science students have a wide range of experience and ability in statistics, which is also difficult to teach in the lecture theatre. For biology students, in particular, a basic understanding of descriptive statistics, using sample data to infer something about a population, and the use of hypothesis testing are essential to making the most of their subject. This is included as the final topic in the St Andrews course and has proved very useful as a precursor to more detailed statistics courses taken in later years. Statistics is part of the second-year biology curriculum in Edinburgh. Since the introduction of the QB workbook, the second-year statistics course has expanded its course notes greatly, although it still relies on lectures rather than self-teaching plus tutorials as the method of instruction.

REFERENCES

Burton, RF (1998) *Biology by Numbers: An encouragement to quantitative thinking*, Cambridge University Press, Cambridge

Davie, AM *et al* (1997) Teaching elementary mathematics to biologists: Lectures or workbooks?, abstract to Conference on Flexible Learning in Tertiary Education, 29–30 September, Napier University, Edinburgh, p 34

APPENDIX 16.1

Workbook example: Proportional relationships to calculate concentrations

Proportional relationships

The simplest form of linear relationship occurs when one of the variables is proportional to the other. This means that when one of the variables changes, the other changes by the same factor.
   At the end of this section you should:

- know what is meant when the relationship between two variables is proportional or inversely proportional;

- be able to draw graphs of data related in these ways;

- be aware of some of the applications of proportional relationships in biology.

We can represent a proportional relationship algebraically as:

$$y = k \cdot x$$

where x and y are the two variables and k is the 'constant of proportionality'. Note that this equation is just the same as that for a straight line:

$$y = bx + a$$

with the intercept $a = 0$. The constant of proportionality k is the same as the slope b.
   For example, the concentration of salt in a given volume of solution is proportional to the amount of salt in that solution. We can represent this as:

$$concentration = \frac{amount}{volume}$$

If the amount of salt is doubled, so too is the concentration. We can rewrite this in the form of a proportional relationship.
Let $x = amount$ and $y = concentration$ and then

$$y = k \cdot x \quad \text{where the constant of proportionality,} \quad k = \frac{1}{volume}$$

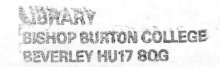

EXERCISE

Sketch the graph relating concentration and amount:

(a) when the volume is 50 ml;
(b) when the volume is 2 litres.

To do this, choose amounts between (say) 1 g and 10 g and work out the concentrations in grams per litre (g.l^{-1}).

(c) What are the units of the slope in each case?

APPENDIX 16.2

Workbook example: graphical analysis of the effect of an insecticide on the fruit fly, in which students use logarithmic transformations of the data.

'Spreading out' data that cover a wide range

Sometimes your experimental data may cover a wide range, such as the following data for the percentage mortality of the fruit fly, *Drosophila melanogaster*, exposed to an insecticide.

Dose (pg)	0	0.1	0.2	0.5	1	2	5	10	20	30
Mortality (%)	0	5	15	40	65	80	90	95	98	99

Suppose you want to find out the dose that kills 50 per cent of the flies (called the LD$_{50}$).
The data are clearly not related linearly (ie in the form of a straight line – biological data rarely are), so the first step is to plot them as shown in the graph at the top.
Note that *data* are *plural*, despite what you may read or hear to the contrary.
In the top graph, note how cramped together the points are at the lower doses, making it very difficult to determine the LD$_{50}$.
One way around this is to plot mortality against the log of the dose. This has been done in the middle of the three graphs. Note how taking logs has 'stretched out' the points on the graph. This makes LD$_{50}$ much easier to determine in the following way.
Read across from the 50 per cent point on the vertical axis (the 'y axis') to the line joining the data points. Then drop a vertical line down from the line through the data to the horizontal axis (the 'x axis'), as shown in the middle graph. Where this vertical line hits the horizontal axis is the log of the dose that kills 50 per cent of the fruit flies. So all we need to do now is to say

  log (LD$_{50}$) = –0.2   (approximately, from the graph)

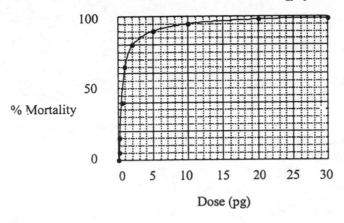

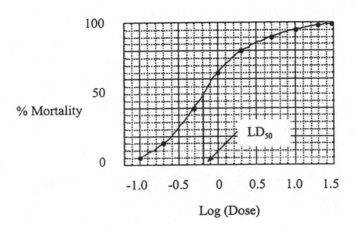

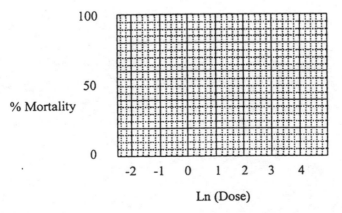

Figure 16.1

so that

$$LD_{50} = 10^{-0.2} = 0.63 \text{ pg}$$

Note that you cannot include the origin (zero) on the horizontal axis because you cannot take the log of zero. The way round this, presentationally, is not to extend the graph to zero, as shown.

Note also that we used common logs here; we could equally well have used natural logs (lns).

EXERCISE

Find out the LD_{50} from the data in the table above using natural logs instead of common logs.

(a) First fill in the blanks in the table below.

Dose (pg)	0	0.1	0.2	0.5	1	2	5	10	20	30
Mortality (%)	0	5	15	40	65	80	90	95	98	99
Ln (dose)	–	-2.30				0.69				3.40

(b) Now, in the bottom graph, plot per cent mortality against the natural logarithm of dose.

(c) Read off ln (LD_{50}) from your graph and convert it to dose in units of pg.

17

Introducing an Interdisciplinary Course

Balasubramanyam Chandramohan

SUMMARY

This chapter focuses on the teaching of a new interdisciplinary degree programme. The specific example cited relates to post-colonial studies, although the basic principles are generalizable to a range of interdisciplinary subjects.

The key argument presented in this chapter is that within the context of discipline-based approaches that dominate the academic scene at the university, interdisciplinary provisions often do not attract the same level of commitment from either staff or students. Often both groups treat them as add-on provisions. Consequently, those responsible for the management of such interdisciplinary programmes must implement special strategies to maintain everyone's interest.

The chapter describes a number of transferable measures that are proving to be very successful.

INTRODUCTION

The University of Luton is one of the 'new' English universities; the institution achieved university status in 1993. As the institution has progressed, very rapidly, from its earlier status as a college of higher education, there has been a substantial increase in the extent and variety of degree provision available to the students. This has been achieved by using the flexibility of a university-wide modular credit scheme. Students accumulate credits for successful completion of modules, and on achievement of the required number of modules ('standard-sized study units') are awarded degrees. While the system encourages the students' right to select modules of their choice, it is only through completion of recognized combinations of modules that specific named awards can be achieved.

One of the significant aspects of the university modular credit scheme is the organization of named awards to provide the following opportunities:

- single discipline awards, for instance BA in History or BSc in Psychology;
- joint awards, such as BA in Linguistics and Literary Studies;
- major, minor combinations, for example BA Politics with History.

The above differentiation depends on the number and combinations of modules completed by the student. The objective in adopting this approach was to offer greater choice of subjects to the students while retaining the coherence of programmes in terms of subject areas covered.

For purposes of the management of delivery, modules are classified into 'fields', and 'field managers' based in particular departments are responsible for organizing the running of the modules which lie within their field. Most fields focus solely on modules grounded within established disciplines; however, there is significant interest in the development of fields which draw upon several disciplines. These emerging fields generally incorporate both multidisciplinary provision (a range of modules in which each is grounded within a specified discipline) and interdisciplinary provision (in which individual modules draw upon material from a range of disciplines to establish academic linkages). (Although we recognize different definitions for the terms multidisciplinary and interdisciplinary, the latter term will be used throughout this case study to refer to both concepts.)

This case study deals with the experience of establishing and managing the field of post-colonial studies.

POST-COLONIAL STUDIES

Post-colonial studies is essentially an interdisciplinary field. It draws on different traditional subject areas such as history, politics, linguistics and literature with the primary purpose of exploring texts and past and contemporary social institutions to consider how these have been affected by the experience of colonialism.

In North American and Australian universities, post-colonial studies is already a well-established area of study. Among British universities it remains in its infancy but is receiving more and more attention, primarily as a post-graduate and research provision. However, undergraduate modules/courses are offered by a growing number universities, such as the University of Kent and the University of Exeter.

The University of Luton has an undergraduate programme in post-colonial studies validated as a field of study which contributes to either joint degrees or the minor portion of major, minor combinations (as described above). These require the students to complete a minimum of nine and six modules from within the post-colonial studies field respectively. (To obtain their honours degree, students are required to complete a total of 24 modules.)

The types of modules in the modular credit scheme (University of Luton, annual) are explained to the students as follows:

- *Core* modules are modules within the subject(s) chosen which *must* be included within the programme of study.

- *Option* modules are modules within the subject(s) chosen which one may choose to study as part of the number required for the programme of study.

- *Elective* modules are modules chosen from elsewhere in the scheme which one wishes to study in addition to the required number of subject modules.

The modules included in the post-colonial studies programme are tabulated in Appendix 17.1. As the programme is not available as a single honours degree, it must be studied with another subject such as management, travel and tourism, business, English or social studies.

The modules cover a range of traditional subject areas that are essentially single-discipline based. The staff who deliver these modules are also drawn from a number of departments in which the primary interest lies with disciplines such as history, linguistics, or literary studies. The attraction of the programme to the students rests on the achievement of understanding of the following issues:

- Ethnicity, difference and 'imagined communities' are attracting increasing attention in contemporary cultural and political debates. The course aims to provide students with a sophisticated understanding of the issues involved.

- Post-colonial studies fosters skills in handling interdisciplinary approaches and multidisciplinary methodology by exposing the students to materials and methods that span more than one academic discipline.

- Students have the opportunity to acquire an in-depth knowledge of societies and cultures of Asia, Africa, the Caribbean and Latin America.

INTERDISCIPLINARITY

Although there can be a no complete division between disciplinary and inter-disciplinary approaches, the dominant ethos within the university (as with most academic institutions) remains that of subject-oriented delivery. Many believe that notions of academic rigour and exactness can more easily be accommodated within an established subject area. Subject-based academic and professional associations cement disciplinary conventions and approaches which, in turn, establish a clear, peer group and niche for the subject. Most particularly, this is manifest through the establishment of a recognized academic vocabulary which is utilized throughout the discipline; recognized definitions and terminology may vary significantly between disciplines. But for interdisciplinary approaches such a standard model is not easily or readily available.

The students who have chosen to work towards the achievement of post-colonial studies degrees (on whom this case study is based) are, thus, affected by two key features of academic environment in the university:

1. The modular system. Since post-colonial studies (for the present) will only be a fraction of the students' workload there is a distinct possibility of the students' primary priorities lying elsewhere. This is particularly the case when taken as the minor element of the degree in which the major may account for as much as three-quarters of the total.

2. The strength of the conventional, discipline-oriented, ethos. Almost by definition, interdisciplinary work requires that a broader perspective be adopted; this can lead to a failure to address matters in the depth achieved by someone with a more narrow focus. Interdisciplinary work gains its strengths by making connections between disciplines. Since most academics operate within a single discipline (even when contributing to interdisciplinary programmes) difficulties can arise if these differences are not appreciated, particularly when assessing the students' performance.

The nature of the subject material is proving a strong attraction for students. It is a key responsibility of the field manager to ensure that the students remain sufficiently inspired to overcome the potential problems outlined above and benefit from the intellectual and methodological inventiveness of interdisciplinarity.

STRATEGIES TO ESTABLISH A STRONG IDENTITY

One factor which characterizes established academic disciplines is a strong identity; history, geography, physics or chemistry (for example) each have well-established identities and this is recognized beyond the discipline itself. Emerging interdisciplinary subjects (such as post-colonial studies) have yet to achieve such recognition even within institutions that offer such subjects.

The tension between disciplinary and interdisciplinary approaches in organizational and pedagogic aspects of the academia is a wider – almost a generic – problem. As Lynn Weber (1998: 3) observes:

One of the greatest threats to knowledge in the modern era is the balkanization of universities into colleges and departments organized around self-contained and ethnocentric academic disciplines . . . [Interdisciplinary ventures] will face enormous obstacles as the intellectual freedom we experience by crossing disciplines also challenges a well entrenched organizational system in higher education.

However, philosophically, disciplinary and inter/postdisciplinary approaches could be seen in a less confrontational, even symbiotic, relationship. Roger Mourad (1997: 102–03) comments:

'. . . in a broader sense, disciplinary and postdisciplinary inquiry would compose a two-way interaction between particular inquiries within disciplines and ideas outside of them. Ideas outside the disciplines impact what knowledge of reality can mean and the ways in which knowledge of reality is pursued, while the latter provide the raw material for the construction of compelling ideas that cut across disciplines. In this way, each side continuously affects the nature of the other.

The two-way dynamics of disciplinarity and interdisciplinarity results, in some institutional contexts, in the acquisition of disciplinary status by interdisciplinary programmes. Funding arrangements, arrangements for teaching and admin-istration (faculties/schools/departments) and research groups help some interdisciplinary initiatives to emerge as subjects/units with strong identities. Philosophical and methodological identities take longer to achieve, while, in the short term, commercial and organizational matters set the pace for transi-tion to the 'respectability' of a disciplinary ethos. In the context of the University of Luton, teaching, learning and research in subject areas such as media studies and travel and tourism nowadays takes place in departmental structures, in the same way as in more traditional subjects – history, literary studies and linguistics, for example.

Post-colonial studies does not yet have a separate administrative structure and is presently located within the Department of Linguistics. In order to survive in a discipline/department-oriented ethos the subject area needs a distinct methodological identity and additional curricular and extra-curricular activities to promote visibility and prestige within the university. The remainder of this case study describes strategies adopted to establish post-colonial studies as a worthwhile and academically rigorous field of study with a strong identity separate from those of its contributing disciplines. Currently, two strategies are being used: running a dedicated discussion forum, and using information technology (IT), especially an e-mail list, to facilitate peer-group and staff–student communication.

Post-colonial studies forum

The forum is a university-wide body for both staff and students interested in post-colonial studies. It meets on a weekly basis on Wednesdays during semesters one and two, when most of the modules in the programme are taught. In these sessions, specialists with different disciplinary and interdisciplinary interests are invited to deliver lectures and lead discussions. The lecture pro-gramme is circulated right at the beginning of each semester. Additionally, each week, the event for the particular week is publicized one–two days in advance. The information is disseminated through notice boards, staff pigeon-holes, 'all-staff' electronic messages, *Campus-Life* magazine and through the post-colonial studies list (see page 154). The publicity material provides informa-tion about the speaker for the particular week, and also invites contributions from all staff and students (see Appendix 17.2).

The weekly lectures have proved to be a success, with students attending a range of sessions not all of which had direct connection with the regions/subjects that they were studying. The lectures have attracted regular attendance by staff members (teaching and non-teaching) from around the university, including the dean of the Faculty of Humanities, who contributed a lecture to the series. The forum lectures have covered a wide range of areas, and included contributions from outside the university. Examples of recent lectures include:

- 'Hong Kong: The "in" and "out" paradigm', Mr Harry Wang, Head of Chinese Centre;

- 'The use of post-colonial literature in teaching ESOL', Mr Ijeoma Bennett Okoli, Department of Linguistics;

- 'Indian media: from post-colonial to global', Dr Daya Kishan Thussu, University of Coventry;

- 'Post-colonial cinema in Africa', Mr Jim Pines, Department of Media Arts;

- 'What do historians think of post-colonial studies?', Dr Larry Butler, Department of History;

- 'Cyprus after British rule', Mr Tim Boatswain, Pro-vice Chancellor (Teaching and Learning) and Dean of Humanities;

- 'The alliance that dare not speak its name: Irish and Afrikaner Nationalists, 1899–1961', Dr Donal Lowry, Oxford Brookes University;

- 'Validating the non-standard: issues of indiginization in world Englishes, Dr Balasubramanyam Chandramohan, Department of Linguistics;

- 'Colonial Ireland: cultural encounters with Ireland's colonial past', Dr John Brannigan, Department of Literary Studies.

The forum meetings were also used as brainstorming sessions to explore more ideas about making post-colonial studies programmes more popular. This has helped to create a sense of identity among both staff and students as well as producing ideas for the future development.

Post-colonial studies list (electronic discussions)

The other initiative was to start a discussion list (post-colonial studies list – PCS list) using the university's e-mail system. All the students were registered with the list to initiate communication and discussion between the students themselves and with the teaching staff. The author moderates the list. In the context of the programme the electronic discussions have an important role in establishing and sustaining a group identity. The list is being used as a source of information, as the staff use it to refer the students to particular educational resources, including information about relevant Web sites. Through the list the students can express their views, seek feedback on their work and critique each other's work. The PCS list creates a less hierarchical platform which facilitates interaction between the staff and the students and between students in different years. In short it is helping to create a 'community of scholars' interested in the subject area of post-colonial studies.

THE FUTURE

The initiatives described above have led to a greater sense of involvement on the part of the students. Meanwhile, both staff and students have noted a raising of the academic prestige of post-colonial studies within the university.

The university is working towards a time when post-colonial studies will be offered as a single honours degree programme in its own right. For those students who choose this opportunity, there will continue to be a need to address matters of interdisciplinarity though issues of prioritization of disciplines will be removed (although they will continue to be a consideration for joint honours and major, minor students).

The attempt to make post-colonial studies a full degree is also appreciated by the students, some of whom are thinking of choosing post-colonial topics for their research dissertations in the final year. The case study ends on a positive note with the post-colonial studies team confident that the ongoing developments will solve the twin problem mentioned above.

REFERENCES

Mourad Jr, R (1997) *Postmodern Philosophical Critique and the Pursuit of Knowledge in Higher Education*, Bergin & Garvey, Westport, CT
University of Luton (Annual) *Modular Credit Scheme Handbook*
Weber, L (1998) Director's comments: Women's studies, an interdisciplinary leader, *Women's Studies: News from Women's Studies at the University of South Carolina*, spring

APPENDIX 17.1

Modules included in the post-colonial studies programme

	Semester 1	Semester 2
Level 1	**MHS28-1 Interdisciplinary Studies: Post-colonialism** EST01-1 Language, Literature and Englishness	**MHS04-1 The Imperial Experience** LIG06-1 Language Variation ISH07-1 National Identities
Level 2	**EST09-2 Language Literature and Colonialism** COL06-2 African Literature in French LIT10-2 Literature and Myth	ISH09-2 Literature of Independence COL05-2 Latin American Fiction LIT13-2 Contemporary Literary Theory 1 PPP26-2 Politics of 'Race' and Immigration CHI34-2 Immigration and Multi-Culturalism PPP27-2 Colonialism and Independence
Level 3	EST10-3 Contemporary Language and Literatures in English CHI32-3 Britain and Decolonization CHI22-3 Insurgencies and Counter-Insurgencies GOG04-3 Exploration, Discovery and Maps EST003 Project/Dissertation (Semesters 1 & 2)	EST22-3 South Asian Literature in Translation EST12-3 African Literature in English ISH23-3 Contemporary Ireland: Modern and Post-colonial PPP59-3 Politics of South Asia MHS22-3 The New Imperialism *c*1860–1914

NOTES

1. This list is being revised for 1999–2000

2. Modules in bold are core modules and are thus compulsory for all students who wish to achieve a named award in post-colonial studies.

APPENDIX 17.2

Publicity material

University of Luton

Post-Colonial Studies Forum

The post-colonial studies forum is essentially an interdisciplinary support provision for the post-colonial studies degrees offered by the Department of Linguistics in the Faculty of Humanities.

However, the forum is also intended to provide a platform for discussion both across disciplines and between students and staff from different faculties. The forum meetings are open to all staff and students in the university.

The post-colonial studies forum uses the following definition of the subject area: 'Post-colonial studies is interdisciplinary in nature and endeavours to bring together fields such as language, literature, culture, history and politics in examining the nature and effect of the experience of colonialism on a wide range of societies.'

The format of presentation at the weekly meetings is usually 40 minutes of lecture and 20 minutes of discussion.

The speakers are generally from within the university and the lectures are delivered on a voluntary basis. There are plans to publish a volume of [selected] presentations as 'Luton Working Papers in Post-Colonial Studies'.

The forum organizes lunchtime lectures on Wednesdays from 1.00 to 2.00 pm on a variety of topics. The venue for this semester's programme is Room A420.

Volunteers who wish to make a presentation at the forum are welcome. Contact details are given below.

Dr Balasubramanyam Chandramohan [or 'Chandra']
Convenor: Post-Colonial Studies Forum
Office: Vicarage Street Building (H313 b)
Internal telephone: ext 2459, fax: 01582 743 466;
e-mail: bala.chandramohan@luton.ac.uk

18

The 'Art' in Introducing Technology to Non-technologists

Ian McPherson

SUMMARY

Working models, often of human beings and animals, have throughout history been used to amaze, frighten and educate. Today automata have evolved into a sophisticated and entertaining kinetic art form with the potential to stimulate a mixture of human senses.

In this chapter, the author has used projects involving the design and construction of kinetic sculpture and 'moving toys' to introduce design students and groups of art teachers on in-service training courses to the principles of mechanics and motion. Additionally it has been found that these topics are excellent as a vehicle for the introduction of problem-based learning (PBL).

Although presented with a focus on technology, the principles illustrated in this chapter are widely transferable as the focus of the author's work is primarily concerned with the removal of the fear associated with the unfamiliar.

INTRODUCTION

Art as a subject in the school curriculum is changing. Three-dimensional design (3D design), including product design and the (design) process involved in the creation of the object are today given their correct important position within the school syllabus. This change has thereby exposed a group of creative and visually mature art school graduate teachers to the fact that for the majority they know little or nothing about 3D design or applied technology.

The author has initiated and participated in a number of continuing professional development (CPD) courses in the area of creative methods in 3D design for both art and technical teachers and it very soon became obvious that one of the first things to be done on these courses was to help some of the participants overcome any 'fear' of technology, technology often being seen as something rigid, only learned from textbooks, something not relevant to a creative subject – something that non-artists use!

METHOD

The following explains some of the approaches used to help to introduce applied technology into the classroom. The approach is by no means unique and acknowledgement is made of the work elsewhere of Robert Race, The Nuffield Curriculum Projects Centre and members of the Education Service of the Museum of Automata, York, among others.

KINETIC ART WORKSHOPS

The typical programme starts with investigation and discussion on the work of established kinetic artists. Emphasis is placed on finding out what means were employed to produce and control the movements that the artist found compelling and essential to his composition. From this the students move into exercises and experimentation using as source the example of mobiles from artists such as Man Ray and Alexander Calder. Use of simple materials such as coat-hanger wire, paper and Plasticine can be enough to introduce the concepts of balance, moment and other factors such as air resistance. The course proceeds to compare and discuss the work of kinetic artists and the very different approaches used by the likes of Jean Tinguely and George Rickey and how their styles could to some degree be likened to the response that may be expected from haptic or visually-minded students.

Closer inspection of the work of George Rickey is used to demonstrate the need for different means of fine tuning the balance of the constructions in order to achieve the slow, almost stately dances that his sculptures perform. Discussions often dwell on the precision, the choice of materials and quality of Rickey's workmanship.

In contrast to Rickey, Jean Tinguely's 'anti-machines' are often seen, initially, as having little or no applied technology, but it may be supposed that is partly the artist's intention.

Kinetic sculpture can also be useful in helping the student to accept the importance of the fourth dimension as an element of 3D composition. This can be seen in designs that have physical forms that alter with function, eg lids and doors that may be opened or closed, forcing the product to be viewed and judged as a continually changing form.

AUTOMATA

The action and intention of much of the kinetic art investigated attempts to be indeterminate – the random movements often being a fortuitous result of the actions of currents of air or water, etc. This type of movement holds a special fascination for the contemporary artist. Automata by contrast are disciplined, the outcome being predetermined and repetitive in action. Tinguely's kinetic, 'méta-matics' – machines that, to the accompaniment of much noise and movement, produce randomly coloured drawings may be compared with the work of Pierre Jaquet-Droz, also Swiss, who in 1774 constructed a mechanical doll worked by cams that could reproduce recognizable drawings of a cupid riding a horse.

Much of historical automata were devised for the owner's pleasure, either public or private. So precise are the mechanisms of these early automata that at 'The First Robot Olympics' at Strathclyde University in 1990 in the competition for robot archery the first prize was won by a 19th-century Japanese archer automaton.

'The archer takes an arrow from the rack, inserts it in his bow, takes aim and fires. This he does four times in succession propelling the arrows approximately 3.8 metres with unrivalled precision, all the while being fanned by two attendant ladies.' (exhibition note, Museum of Automata, York).

The history of automata with its roots going back as far as the ancient Greeks is in itself a subject worthy of much investigation, but it is modern automata that the author feels is particularly relevant as a source of stimuli for an introduction to applied technology.

Automata are still being made today, and in recent years a new breed of 3D artists has taken the ideas of the likes of Heath-Robinson and Roland Ematt a few stages further, endowed their constructions with the spirit of the cartoon, of seaside postcards and 'end-of-the-pier show'. These artists often, in addition, strip away all pretence of secrecy of means and expose the mechanisms for all to see. Purists may decry this demystification of the automata, however for the viewer, be they teacher or pupil, the cause and effect of cogs, cams and assorted linkages are there to be both understood and enjoyed for their own sake.

AUTOMATA WORKSHOPS

'A mechanism is a system or structure of moving parts that perform a function.' With this working definition, the emphasis for the workshop is on mechanisms that change one form of movement into another.

As a starting point, hand-powered household kitchen appliances and utensils are investigated and through describing the purpose and analysing the different movements of such artefacts as pedal bins, egg-whisks and nutcrackers, basic principles may be observed. Often a search around the classroom or personal effects exposes such apparently unlikely candidates such as pencil sharpeners, lock and keys even ball-point pens.

Initially, observational drawings with explanatory arrows and other graphic devices record the mechanical intentions of the device and from such sketches card models are used to demonstrate the type of motion involved.

Simple cardboard, scrap and sticky-tape sketch models, in the true spirit of the BBC children's television programme 'Blue Peter', are used in preference to construction kits such as 'Fishertechnics' for a number of reasons:

- there is little or no cost in 'found objects';

- because of 'technophobia' associated with construction kits;

- with sketch models all that is produced is part of the student's own creation.

From card models the class may proceed to simple wooden automata/toys and although existing examples are shown during the introduction, it is important that the students be in control of the concept. For this reason they are asked to design and construct their own creations rather than make to a set-piece drawing.

The students have a number of decisions to make at this the concept stage, such as:

- Are we trying to mimic the movement of people and animals; or will it be an abstract composition perhaps trying to convey emotion through the movement?

- What movement are we intending to have? (This may be expressed in analogous terms such as swooping, wriggling, happy, sad, etc.)

- Will each of the movements be dependent on a separate source of power or input or can they be combined so one component will impart an action into another? (the preferred route).

- How can we achieve the intended movement?

Group brainstorming sessions at this point have proved to be beneficial, with suggestions being both wacky and wonderful. The resulting kinetic creations (Figure 18.1) are found to be both aesthetically and technically valid.

PROBLEM-BASED LEARNING (PBL) IN DESIGN

Design projects may vary in length and academic demand. They can range from short intensive topic-specific projects to long-term, major events with extensive research and validation demands. Design projects also allow for the increasing theoretical content of the programme or module to be integrated where appropriate and the relevance of the content be demonstrated in a practical manner.

PBL is used to inspire and to engage students in deeper cognitive study and to give them responsibility for their own learning.

There are three major roles for PBL within the design syllabus. They are:

- the acquisition of factual knowledge;
- the mastery of general principles or concepts that can be transferred to solve similar problems;
- the acquisition of examples that may be used in future problem-solving situations of a similar nature.

The PBL methods used fall into two main categories: (i) set briefs composed of 'wicked' or 'ill-structured problems'; (ii) self-select projects. Elements common to both are:

Figure 18.1 *Kinetic sculpture/toy: turn the wheel and the shapes writhe around.*
© *Napier University*

- Students require more information than is presented to them. The information or given material or scenario may also be alien to them, thus forcing the student to investigate and conduct primary research.

- The problem focus and demands change as information is found, thus engaging the student or group in project management and decision making.

- There is no right way nor fixed formula for conducting the investigations. Each problem is unique and there is (usually) no single correct answer.

WORKING FROM SET BRIEFS

Set projects give opportunities for creativity within parameters set by staff, open competition brief or outside agencies.

All students in the cohort are assigned carefully structured and prescribed projects. This allows for a basis from which to assess the problems and procedures of basic design and its plural outcomes.

The given brief may be 'wicked' in nature in so much as the student will be unable to access appropriate background information or data on the topic. Such is the case in the widely-used device of the problem of building bridges out of spaghetti pasta (see Figure 18.2). In addition to designing the form of

Figure 18.2   *Problem-solving exercise, pasta bridges.* © *Napier University*

the bridge the student must first embark on an investigation into the physical properties of the defined building material. 'Wicked' problems encourage a holistic approach to the problem, often require lateral thinking, and result in deeper understanding of the essence of design discipline.

Set projects in later years of the BSc Industrial Design programme require the students to respond to demands that reflect the balance of design and technology within the programme. The briefs used can often be open-ended. That is they are constructed usually by giving a scenario or situation and is usually stated without naming a definite article as a design outcome.

By using scenarios rather than requesting a particular defined design outcome or artefact, a greater and more creative range of proposals is generated. By way of simple example, the following is offered: If one is asked to 'design a chair' the solution offered may simply be no more than a platform to sit on, four legs to maintain the platform at the 'correct' (?) height and something to 'support' (?) the back: in fact a chair! But a chair without purpose.

However, if the brief were to ask one to: 'Design an artefact or device to support the body at an attitude suited to the correct posture for, say, typing, or eating or lazing in the sun', the student/designer immediately has to start asking further questions, eg: who will use it?, where will they use it?, when will they use it?, what will it cost?, how will it be made?

The answers to these questions will, in turn, lead to further questions and ultimately a more complete solution and a deeper approach to learning in general.

SELF-SELECT PROJECTS

In the senior years of the undergraduate industrial design programme the opportunity given to the students to select their own project topic allows them to take responsibility for their own learning and the content of their portfolio.

Self-select projects are aimed at giving students choice. Here parameters have to be justified, set and defined by the students themselves, the final approval and go-ahead of the teaching staff having to be earned. By having to research and set appropriate aims and criteria and providing creative solutions to them, intellectual demands commensurate with an honours degree course are established. The more able student is also offered the opportunity to demonstrate greater independent thinking, and intellectual and creative capacity.

In evaluating a project's acceptability within the framework of student-centred learning, the following criteria are applied:

- it should be within the sphere of industrial design;

- it should be academically rigorous;

- it should be acceptable to supervisors;

- it should be capable of being assessed.

The routes to deciding the topic and content of the major self-select project are for the student many and varied.

An acquired interest in PBL and memories of a disinterested and frustrated time in the elementary school science class led one final-year undergraduate to design a modular laboratory microscope (see Figure 18.3). The redesigned product is centred upon an attempt to appeal to the child user by offering the opportunity for added 'involvement' in the learning process. The concept allows the pupil to configure the microscope for a variety of fieldwork uses. Through its form it also has the capability of demonstrating the underlying physics principles involved.

In the case of the portable vet's ultrasonic scanner (Figure 18.4) the 'need' was established following an industrial placement with a company specializing in ultrasonic equipment. Involvement with the company sparked off in the student an enquiry into possible new markets of ultrasonic scanners. Upon graduating the student returned to the company in a permanent capacity.

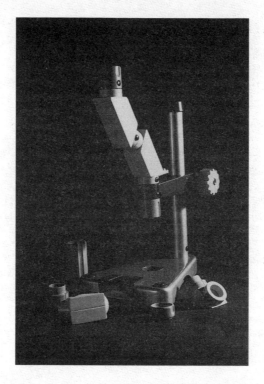

Figure 18.3   *Modular microscope for elementary schools.* © *Napier University*

THE PROBLEMS AND REWARDS OF MAINTAINING A PBL REGIME

Students, or indeed staff, coming from a lecture and book learning background may feel uncomfortable about conducting open research, working in groups, etc. Some may initially be so uncomfortable with the concept that they request that a (predicted) solution be named or identified. These students are usually the product of a strict 'know that' rather than a 'know how' school environment and will require an additional amount of nurturing by class tutors.

Implementing PBL requires above all a dedicated team of teaching staff who are prepared invest time and effort to engage, with passion, the task of coaxing, mentoring and accepting the student's point of view and acknowledging that the student has ownership of the situation. All of this is time consuming for staff who must conduct regular moderating meetings, coordinate tutorials, etc. The rewards for the teacher are enormous as it enables them to work among students who see education as being meaningful and rewarding.

It has often be said that the best advertisement for the Napier BSc Industrial Design Programme and display of evidence of good teaching practice is the students and graduates themselves. Through the use of PBL they come to regard

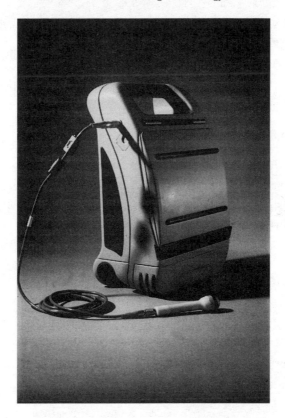

Figure 18.4 *Portable ultrasonic scanner. © Napier University*

the course as their course, and feel that they have a stake in the continuing pursuit of excellence upon graduation.

CONCLUSION

The approach described in this paper is not in any way to be seen as an attempt at replacing traditional methods of introducing technology, however in practice it has proved to be very successful within the confines of the specialist area of art education and other allied disciplines such as industrial or product design and stands to be judged by observing:

- the satisfaction expressed by those taking part;
- the quality of the completed work;
- the successful and appropriate integration of technology within the work;

- the student's ability to come to terms with and to apply, initially by trial and error, the basic principles of technology;

- the student's willingness to seek out the 'why' following the 'how';

- the enjoyment and delight shown by the participants in continuing to extend the amount of knowledge gained even after the course has finished;

- the willingness of the in-service participants to incorporate the knowledge gained into their own classroom.

Should more theory be introduced into the early sessions or on in-service courses? On this matter the author is, as yet, undecided, but due to the duration and intention of these classes he is tempted to continue with the present philosophy of giving answers to any enquiries, emphasizing, where appropriate, that the information given should be seen merely as a pointer to where more knowledge is to be found.

ACKNOWLEDGEMENTS

The author would like to note the help and assistance given to him in the preparation of this paper by Sandy Turner, Queen Anne High School, Dunfermline, and the staff of The Museum of Automata, York, England.

FURTHER READING

Caborn, C *et al* (1989) *Design and Technology*, Nelson, Surrey, UK
Hillier, M (1988) *Automata and Mechanical Toys*, Bloomsbury, London, UK
Kranz, C (1974) *Science and Technology in The Arts*, Van Nostrand, New York, USA
Lowenfeld, V (1987) *Creative and Mental Growth*, Prentice-Hall, Berkelely, USA
Robertson, A (1992) *Museum of Automata* (catalogue)
Selz, P (1970) *Directions in Kinetic Sculpture*, University of California, Berkeley, USA

19

Editors' Concluding Comments

Stephen Fallows and Kemal Ahmet

This final section summarizes the various approaches used within this book. Although the methods employed have been essentially in connection with teaching and learning of essential but non-mainstream subjects, there is no reason why these successful techniques for inspiring students should not be employed elsewhere. Further, the spreading and transference of ideas and techniques both within and between disciplines should be strongly encouraged.

In any course, module, lecture and whenever effective learning is required, clear aims and objectives are essential and provide student motivation. 'What are the expected learning outcomes?' is a question that every teacher should ask (and be able to answer) before the commencement of any teaching and learning session.

Without exception, methods employed in this book support the view that learning is most effective when student involvement, participation and inter-action is maximized. To encourage active participation, a useful tip is to be less discriminatory of student input at the beginning of a course, 'tightening-up' on a gradual basis. Student inspiration is closely connected with the tutor's enthusiasm, genuine excitement and love of the subject; strategic use of gentle humour (not merely telling jokes) can be very effective in generating inspiration. Especially with non-central subjects, constant encouragement and reminders of the importance and relevance of the subject, together with pertinent, specific examples, are powerful motivators. The tutor in the role of facilitator and encourager – a trusted 'coach' rather than a distant 'director' is most welcome by learners, although it must be emphasized that lecturer expertise is essential and there cannot be a substitute for subject experience and specialism.

Students generally dislike being 'lectured at' and loathe the unnecessary use of jargon. Avoiding unnecessary terminology in teaching (for example) the traditionally disliked subject of statistics and discussing data analysis under the heading 'Another 20 ways to cock up a research project' is likely to fuel inspiration. Appropriately worded titles, incidentally, can be very useful in generating inspiration. The physics tutorial entitled 'Experimentil Erors' never fails to catch attention, although students have complained about poor spelling! Similarly, topics for statistical investigation such as 'Is chocolate an adequate

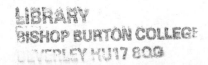

substitute for sex?', or 'How much alcohol is required before male and female students vomit?' are bound to arouse great interest in the biology student, while the resulting data and analyses are likely to be as valid as any other 'traditional' topic.

Group learning has been a recurring theme within this book. That working and learning in pairs and small groups is highly desirable for effective and exciting learning should be emphasized to students. Unfortunately, many students, perhaps because of the preoccupation with formal examination 'working in isolation' mentality, feel that learning should be a solo activity and frequently fail to exploit the enormous benefits of learning in groups.

Learners always appreciate rapid feedback following assessment. Although not always appropriate, it is well worth designing objective tests for at least some of the assessed work. The fast marking enables students quickly to learn details of their performance. With full feedback, students are able to reflect on their strengths as well as finding out about their weaknesses.

Preferred learning methods vary enormously between individuals, so variety is important in formal situations. Disinterest may be a reflection of an ineffective teaching style. Teaching materials should be presented using a variety of methods. Wholesale use of even high-technology methods can bore or 'switch off' learners. Some students prefer reading and writing, while others learn more effectively from visual presentation. Talking and listening is most effective for some, and use of 'hands-on' is yet another effective method. Clearly, employing a variety of learning styles is bound to be appreciated by the majority of learners.

A negative comment sometimes heard from the lecturer is that students are uninterested, or that they lack ability, and this is unfortunately associated with occasional sarcasm, leading to mistrust by the learner. In a position of authority, the lecturer's role is to believe in the students, and to act as an effective catalyst for learning. Irrespective of the course material and students' background, the tutor must make the assumption that all learners have the potential to become inspired and to develop a passion for learning. It is the tutor's responsibility to be sensitive to students' needs and to present materials in a variety of methods to best meet individual learning styles, and to find techniques of presenting material in exciting ways. The feeling that the material is not relevant to the learner's life experiences often causes lack of student interest. Personalizing material can convert dry, uninspiring material into forms that illustrate meaning and importance. Materials need to be practical, allowing students to focus on topics and issues relevant to their personal interests. For example, mature students are happier where assignments allow them to report on their professional work and explore issues relevant to their daily activities. Openness, honesty and a genuine concern for students' learning are always appreciated; caring, supporting environments induce motivation. Students are invariably inspired when their ideas are genuinely listened to, and when there is fast response to their queries, be it direct or via e-mail, telephone message or fax.

Effective learning can result in a wide range of situations, formal or otherwise. One problem with the traditional lecture is that especially within certain subject areas, the optimum speed of delivery may be difficult to judge. For example, in teaching mathematics to non-specialists, some learners inevitably find the material too easy while others find the pace too brisk, both sets of students 'switching off' for different reasons. In certain courses, lectures have been abandoned in favour of other methods, enabling the individual to be responsible for the learning and the pace. Well-designed workbooks, together with supporting tutorials and self-help groups have been successfully used for replacing lectures. Such set-ups are used, for example, for teaching mathematics to non-specialists, enabling the learners to work at their own speed. The idea of students helping each other is very powerful and should be promoted as frequently as possible. Workbooks with a 'reflective diary' page at the end of each section can be helpful: where the learner completes and hands it in, this can provide valuable feedback about student feelings. In some courses, students are asked to keep journals, helping them to think more deeply about course content. The contents can be very revealing about the strengths and weaknesses of a particular course.

Experiential learning, where variations of the Kolb experiential learning cycle can be employed, results from undergoing a particular experience followed by reflection and extrapolation of learning. The emphasis again is on student-centred learning. Experiential learning can occur through 'real' situations as well as by using 'simulations'. Students of architecture making measurements of physical parameters while experiencing their own living environment provide one category of experiential learning. On the other hand, simulations can be used in many subject areas (eg chemistry and business), providing a powerful way of getting students involved instead of 'just turning up and sitting passively'. With the use of state-of-the-art computer packages, simulations can be extremely realistic. Experiential learning through simulations is often considered to be fun and a welcome change from traditional lecture-based teaching. And clearly, the retention of knowledge and skills increases as the amount of experiential activity increases. This results in deeper learning than conventional approaches. Although, as in all learning situations, the key aims and objectives have to be made clear at the outset, students often find that the material only begins to make sense once they start reflecting on their experiences.

Problem solving and investigative work are recognized to inspire students and ensure student-centredness. Problem-based learning is often used for deeper cognitive study, giving students the responsibility for their own learning. Use of authentic problems and collaborative learning techniques helps enormously in the learning process, where the learning activities are often anchored to a larger task. Engaging students in solving relevant, often intriguing and bizarre, but authentic case problems in cooperative work-groups and using problem-based learning to emulate the work-place help to capture and develop the student interest. In certain situations, learning is on a 'need to know' basis, where students assimilate factual knowledge, discover how to analyze problems, ask good questions and retrieve information, and learn how to become self-directed learners. Not an easy option, problem-based learning situations require dedicated, passionate teachers to coax and mentor the students, accepting their points of view and acknowledging that learners have ownership of the situation. In contrast, in the traditional classroom students may simply watch, memorize and repeat information. In teaching any subject, materials that necessitate students having to engage in mindless memorization should be avoided.

In certain approaches, teamwork is encouraged in self-designated work areas, creating a feeling of belonging. Teachers provide support to the teams but students are persuaded to use teammates as their first source of information and assistance. In situations where students are more self-directed and take charge of their learning, the teacher's role is decentralized; the students are viewed as proactive participants metacognitively, motivationally and behaviourally. It is sometimes felt that certain student 'types' (eg engineers) are not particularly communicative, so teamwork is even more beneficial. In student-centred learning, teachers should encourage the students to have team meetings, communicate ideas, listen actively, negotiate actions and resolve conflicts and ensure that every student contributes in writing where team assignments are set.

Contrary to traditionalist views, 'academic' subjects can be taught in the student-centred classroom, promoting active learning. Instead of formal examinations, students are sometimes asked to produce course dossiers (journals), freewriting in their journals both before and after the class, producing a critique based on the concepts they have come to understand. Students may also participate in rating the performance of each of the group members. Freewriting can be used to help students learn how to learn and to apply what they learn, rather than memorizing what some expert has established. Freewriting helps students to move to higher orders of learning, ensuring understanding of concepts rather than viewing the material as an accumulation of random facts and figures. Requiring full commitment, tutors must support and challenge the learners' thinking while encouraging the testing of ideas against alternative views and contexts. Students appreciate environments where they are allowed to articulate verbally, collaborate with peers, share knowledge and negotiate a meaningful response to the problem set, and where there exists focused mentoring by a specialist in the field. Where case studies are used, enthusiasm is improved when the material is structured to have a developmental nature. In splitting the case into various components, the students are then able to relate to the unifying thread.

Ownership is powerful in providing inspiration. Where students in science are required to collect their own (unique) data, interest, motivation and curiosity are greatly improved. Motivation also increases where the learner is given ownership of the process used to develop a solution and is supported in developing ownership of the task. Ownership can result from requiring students to undertake small pieces of research of their own choosing. Analysis of own data is not confined to the sciences. In teaching management to mature students, learning is more effective where the data is derived from ones own place of employment: 'Some had spent a long time finding it, but it was their own data! Analyses are more fruitful as students establish ownership'.

Any successful approach should recognize the wealth of knowledge students already possess. In any situation, the learning taking place depends heavily on students' prior knowledge and experience. Traditionally, students fail to apply what has been taught to the real world, so emphasis on transferability is important. Where the findings of group projects were published for consideration by a professional audience in one course, student motivation was increased: their work was being taken seriously by the outside world.

Learners are always inspired by examples of how (abstract) principles are applied in real life by real people in real situations. Students, especially in traditionally 'abstract' subjects, are enthused by real examples, tangible to their world. Being taught to work out accounts in relation to the home and the family in a mathematics appreciation course is far more motivating than, as one student put it, 'the drudgery of trying to complete copious amounts of stupid problems'. In teaching theoretical concepts (eg mechanics and motion) to designers, the students can construct real examples through practical projects, resulting in dynamic models. Commonly, *ad hoc* techniques are used, but students gradually accept that basic scientific principles have to be applied.

In inspiring students, 'Tell me and I forget, show me and I remember, involve me and I understand' is well worth remembering.

Contact Details

The case studies included in this book have all been created by practitioners in higher education for the benefit of colleagues throughout the worldwide community of higher education.

It is increasingly the case that the primary mode of communication within the international higher education community is by means of e-mail. This mode has been utilized extensively throughout the development of this book; for many authors, the sole mode of communication with the editors has been via e-mail. Since e-mail is a preferred and rapid mode of communication for our contributing authors we list the e-mail addresses of all contributors overleaf. For readers who prefer to use more traditional communications routes, postal addresses are given also.

Chapter	Contributing author	Academic institution	E-mail address	Contact address
Chapters 1, 2 and 19	Kemal Ahmet, Stephen Fallows	University of Luton	kemal.ahmet@luton.ac.uk stephen.fallows@luton.ac.uk	University of Luton Luton Bedfordshire LU1 3JU England
Chapter 3	Calvin S Kalman	Concordia University	kalman@vax2.concordia.ca	Concordia University Montreal Quebec H3G 1M8 Canada
Chapter 4	Peter Ommundsen	Selkirk College	ommundsen@selkirk.bc.ca	Selkirk College Castlegar British Colombia V1N 3J1 Canada
Chapter 5	John R Savery	DePaul University	jsavery@condor.depaul.edu	DePaul University 2350 N Kenmore Avenue Chicago, IL 60614 USA
Chapter 6	Mark W Teale	University of Lincolnshire and Humberside	markt@staff.humber.ac.uk	University of Lincolnshire and Humberside Cottingham Road Kingston upon Hull HU6 7RT England
Chapter 7	Andréa Riesch Toepell	Brock University	atoepell@attcanada.net	Brock University St Catherines Ontario L2S 3A1 Canada
Chapter 8	Jonathan Lean, Terry Mangles and Jonathan Moizer	University of Plymouth	j.lean@plymouth.ac.uk t.mangles@plymouth.ac.uk j.moizer@plymouth.ac.uk	University of Plymouth Plymouth Devon PL4 8AA England

Chapter	Contributing author	Academic institution	E-mail address	Contact address
Chapter 9	Susan Nichols	Flinders University	sue.nichols@flinders.edu.au	Flinders University PO Box 2100 Adelaide, SA 5000 Australia
Chapter 10	Carol Primrose	ex University of Glasgow	primrose@torvean.u-net.com	15 Brackenbrae Road Bishopbriggs Glasgow G64 2BS Scotland
Chapter 11	A C Lynn Zelmer	Central Queensland University	l.zelmer@cqu.edu.ac	Central Queensland University Rockhampton Queensland 4702 Australia
Chapter 12	Josefina Alvarez	New Mexico State University	jalvarez@nmsu.edu	New Mexico State University Las Cruces New Mexico 88003 USA
Chapter 13	Anne Arnold and John Truran	University of Adelaide	aarnold@economics.adelaide.edu.au jtruran@arts.adelaide.edu.au	University of Adelaide Adelaide South Australia 5005 Australia
Chapter 14	Graham Clarke	University of Wales – Bangor	g.clarke@bangor.ac.uk	University of Wales Bangor Gwynedd LL57 2UW Wales

Chapter	Contributing author	Academic institution	E-mail address	Contact address
Chapter 15	John Flynn	University of Lincolnshire and Humberside	johnf@staff.humber.ac.uk	University of Lincolnshire and Humberside Cottingham Road Kingston upon Hull HU6 7RT England
Chapter 16	Philip Hammond and Jim Aiton	University of St Andrews	psh2@st-and.ac.uk jfa@st-and.ac.uk	University of St Andrews St Andrews Fife KY16 9TS Scotland
	Gareth Hughes and Ian Nimmo	University of Edinburgh	gareth.hughes@ed.ac.uk ian.nimmo@ed.ac.uk	University of Edinburgh Edinburgh EH8 9BE Scotland
Chapter 17	Balasubramanyam Chandramohan	University of Luton	bala.chandramohan@luton.ac.uk	University of Luton Luton Bedfordshire LU1 3JU England
Chapter 18	Ian McPherson	Napier University	i.mcpherson@napier.ac.uk	Napier University Colinton Road Edinburgh EH14 1DJ Scotland

Index